The Wood & Canvas Canoe

The Wood & Canvas Canoe

A Complete Guide to its History, Construction, Restoration, and Maintenance

Jerry Stelmok and Rollin Thurlow

Tilbury House, Publishers

Gardiner, Maine

Library of Congress Cataloging-in-Publication Data

Stelmok, Jerry.
    The wood & canvas canoe.

    1. Canoes and canoeing. I. Thurlow, Rollin, 1948-
II. Title. III. Title: Wood and canvas canoe.
VM353.S78   1987   623.8'29   87-80698

ISBN 0-88448-046-1

Portions of this book first appeared in *WoodenBoat.*

Designed on Crummett Mountain by Edith Allard
Composition by High Resolution, Camden, Maine
Printing and binding by Quebecor/Book Press,
Brattleboro, Vermont

10 9 8 7 6

Library of Congress Catalog Card Number: 87-80698
ISBN: 0-88448-046-1

Tilbury House, Publishers
132 Water Street
Gardiner, Maine 04345

In memory of Francis E. (Mick) Fahey (1906-1985), whose knowledge, patience, and wisdom guided many to a keener perception and fuller appreciation of the great outdoors.

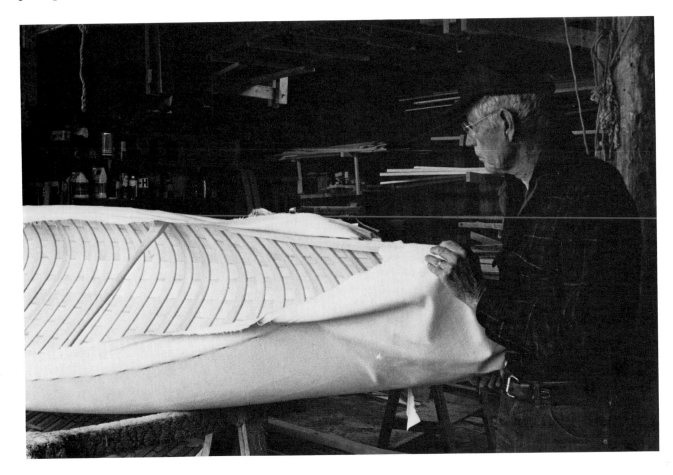

Contents

Acknowledgements

Our wives Debbie and Andrea deserve the credit for enabling us to complete this book, through their many years of patience, support, and encouragement. Seldom did they pressure us to take on respectable jobs, and for this they have our deepest love and appreciation.

Special thanks must also go to Garret Conover for providing so many of the photographs, and to our friend Roger Normand, who processed the film and kept us on schedule. Also in this category belong Henri Vallancourt, Bill Riviere, Jeff and Jill Dean of the Wooden Canoe Heritage Association, Ruth Gray, Steve Krautkremer of Old Town Canoe, and George White — friends and experts whose help can not possibly be properly acknowledged in this brief section.

Many others opened their libraries, dug into their files and photo albums — not to mention their memories — and made contributions for which we are most grateful. Without them, this book would be much leaner and our understanding of the canoe's development very sketchy. These include Guy Cyr, Dave Baker, Ken Solway, Charles King, Jack McGreivey, Herbert Hartmen, Bart Hauthaway, Henry Gerrish, James Gerrish, Constance Sawtell, Tim Bacon, Lila and Lawrence McKelvey, Laurence "Pop" Moore, Kenny Wheaton, Sonney Sprague, Joel Fawcett, Walter Elliott, Florance Sprague, Mona Watson, The Bill Miller family, Bronson Trever, Phil DeLorme, Louis Arsenault, Harmon Poole Jr., Arthur M. Bodin, Dana Hinckley, and Willard Millis.

The individuals of the following organizations were extremely helpful in providing research material and photographs: Marilyn Gass, Bangor Historical Society; Steve Brooks, Maine State Museum; Bonnie Collins and Patty Bouchard, Maine State Library; Ralph Notaristefano, Traditional Small Craft Association; Anne Bray and Cynthia Curtis, *WoodenBoat Magazine*; Hallie Bond, Adirondack Museum; Ben Fuller, Mystic Seaport Museum; Daniel Holbrook, Charles River Museum of Industry; and the staff of the Bangor and Old Town Public Libraries.

Canoe study plans are by Rollin Thurlow, illustrations by Jerry Stelmok. Unless otherwise indicated, photographs are by the authors. The frequent credits marked simply, GC, belong to Garret Conover.

Foreword

Until recently I had known Jerry Stelmok and Rollin Thurlow only casually. I was well aware of their reputations as master canoe builders and restorers and, of course, Jerry's book *Building the Maine Guide Canoe* is in my library. I had chatted with both of them (always an enlightening experience) at various canoe meetings such as the annual canoe show sponsored by the Penobscot Paddle and Chowder Society at Bangor and at assemblies of the Wooden Canoe Heritage Association. On occasion, also, we corresponded.

It was not until Rollin began to delve into the history of Maine's canoe builders that I grew to know him better when, on several occasions, he visited my home so that we could prowl through my files for missing bits out of the past.

But I came to know Rollin and Jerry best when the publisher of *The Wood & Canvas Canoe* sent me a copy of their manuscript. With perceptive editorial foresight, he included sections which had been edited by the authors. The typed pages were liberally sprinkled with tiny between-the-lines scrawls indicating dissatisfaction with the original copy by the authors. The late Somerset Maugham, noted English author, once said: "Only a mediocre writer is always at his best." A writer who is unhappy with his copy and who plies a blue pencil to improve it is, indeed, not a mediocre writer. I was pleased to see the copious editing of the manuscript, a sure sign of meticulous attention to detail.

Perhaps this is what best characterizes *The Wood & Canvas Canoe*. During Rollin's research into the history of Maine's canoe builders (difficult at best since they left virtually no literature nor records), no tidbit of history, however insignificant it might seem to a layman, was deemed unimportant. He kept digging and he continues to dig. Thanks to his efforts much of what had been veiled in the haze of passing years is now recorded within the pages of *The Wood & Canvas Canoe*.

But history is only a part of this book. The extensive "how-to" segments reveal the same exacting dedication to detail. It is as if Jerry Stelmok wore a microphone as he built a canoe and recorded not only his techniques but also his thoughts. When he chooses white cedar over red he explains the reason for his choice. When specialized tools are not available at the hardware store, he improvises and advises on how the reader can do the same. He describes minutely the materials required, the fastenings, the fabrics. In fact, *The Wood & Canvas Canoe* could well become a shop manual for anyone seeking to set up a canoe-building or -restoring business.

Shop manuals can be pretty dull reading, however. But not *The Wood & Canvas Canoe*. Bits of Yankee humor pop up unexpectedly. Occasionally, too, as a sort of natural extension of the canoe's reason of being, there are refreshing notes about deer in the fields near Jerry's shop. Briefly he describes the mating flight of woodcock, or a pair of black ducks patrolling the farm pond.

All in all, *The Wood & Canvas Canoe* is a complete book — literally. The reader will learn of the canoe's origin, its evolvement into the present, how to build or restore it, and even how best to enjoy it. It takes time for a book to become a classic in its field. I think that is the destiny of *The Wood & Canvas Canoe* — but I believe it will attain that status sooner rather than later.

Bill Riviere
North Berwick, Maine

Introduction

Time spent in a wooden canoe of fine lines and able handling qualities is intoxicating. Restoring vintage canoes or building such craft from scratch can be consuming. It will ruin a man or a woman for any other work. This is not to dismiss all canoe builders as rapscallions, curmudgeons, or reprobates. But in the majority of cases there are the symptoms of an addiction, or at least a suspension of common sense where canoes are concerned. We are kin to the hard-bitten trout fisherman who stands out in the wind and rain breaking ice from the guides of his fly rod for a chance at an early season rainbow, or the railbird unable to resist the summons of the bugle, knowing it will be followed by the starting gun which will launch the thoroughbreds from the gates. We all know better, yet we simply can't help ourselves. Why else would we devote our most productive years attempting to revive an industry that has not known real prosperity since before the Great Depression? Today, at long last, wooden canoes and their construction are enjoying a quiet renaissance, and this only encourages us, adding fuel to our dreams.

The authors have been captivated by the magic of canoes since childhood. One, the son of a dairy farmer with feet planted firmly on dry land, could think of practically nothing else after the age of 12. With money saved haying, he purchased, against the prayers of his very understanding parents, a wounded and bleeding 18' Kennebec guides model canoe. This aristocrat fallen upon hard times, stripped of its deeply checked canvas, and reinforced with an armor of fiberglass, would patiently teach him the basics of canoemanship during dozens of modest excursions on local waters, outings which were to him as exciting as a passage to Hudson's Bay.

The other was more formally inducted into the world of travel by wooden canoe, learning by example, straining growing muscles to set a loaded canoe with a fellow scout in the bow safely down a pitch on Maine's Allagash. Golden memories of these early adventures brewed a love for this freedom, leading him back to the rivers whenever possible throughout high school, college, and the service.

This common passion, still not precisely defined, brought us together at a school for boatbuilders, located at that time in a stalwart former lifeboat sation on wind- and wave-battered West Quoddy Head, the easternmost point of the nation. Before we left the school, a good friend and teacher would launch us together into an improbable enterprise actually building the canoes we had previously only paddled.

Since then, together and separately we have built, repaired, and restored hundreds of canoes, taken lines from dozens, drawn up plans, built forms, conducted workshops, and probed deeply into the murky past of the wood canvas canoe. In the pages ahead we hope to share with the reader much of what we have learned in the process. In doing so, we hope further to impart a small portion of the essence of these wonderful craft that goes beyond cedar and canvas, tacks and bolts — the enchantment of boats so well adapted to the moods of our waterways, they seem a part of them.

The Wood
& Canvas
Canoe

Birchbark Origins   1

We have the Indians to thank for the wood-canvas canoe. From the woodlands around them, using only the simplest of tools, these master builders gathered all their materials and fashioned lovely, functional craft that were the direct predecessors of the relatively modern canvas-covered variety. The portable and durable birchbark shells, reinforced with ribs and planking of cedar, made them masters of their forested, waterway-laced domains. Nothing nearly as elegant or versatile was developed by cultures in other parts of the world with similar climate and terrain, though in many cases the materials were at hand and the need obvious.

The highly refined birch canoes of the Northeastern Indian tribes in particular served as the inspiration to a handful of resourceful Yankees who, faced with a shortage of the native canoes, borrowed heavily from them for construction and design details as well as styling when developing the first wood-canvas models. Steeped in the new skills of industrialization, and armed with wood sense and a clever ingenuity, the Yankees transformed the one-of-kind birch prototypes into practical craft that could be readily mass-produced to exacting specifications. The blend of ages-old woodscraft of the Native Americans and Yankee common sense resulted in a watercraft that was purely American in concept and building technique, while most other craft were at best adaptations of existing European boatbuilding technology.

Although one needn't know how to build a birchbark canoe in order to build one of wood and canvas, some knowledge of the birchbark's construction and materials can be helpful. An understanding of the Indian bark canoe certainly enriches any prospective builder with an appreciation of the canoe's distinguished heritage.

There are few builders of birchbark canoes today, and of these few, only three or four are consistently building well-made canoes in the traditional manner. Luckily for me, when I decided to learn more about this fascinating craft, after first poring over *The Bark Canoes and Skin Boats of North America* by Adney and Chapelle, I needed only slip across the border into New Hampshire and look up a friend I'd gotton to know over the past few years.

Henri Vaillancourt

Greenville, New Hampshire, seems an unlikely spot to find the world's foremost birchbark canoe builder. The ordinary frame houses perch along the hilly streets like mussels on a ledge, seemingly ready to domino into the river that runs through this typical small New England milltown. Jobs in the textile mills haven't completely dried up here, as in many of Greenville's sister towns, but the young people with an eye toward prosperity either move elsewhere, or face commuting to high-paying jobs associated with the high-tech industries that have sprouted along Route 128 north of Boston; it is the northward sprawl of this computer-based culture rather than the traditional industries that promise the region future vitality.

Henri Vaillancourt's father worked to retirement in the mills, his mother still lives in Greenville, and although Henri has chosen to remain in his home town, his work and interests are far removed from the pace of this mid-New England community. For the past 16 years he has been self-employed, meticulously building birchbark canoes mainly after the designs of the Abenaki Indians of Maine and New Brunswick. His interest in the cultures of Native North Americans has led him to research among the Cree and the Montagnais of far northern Mistassini and Ungava, and prompted him to launch a non-profit trust dedicated to preserving the material cultures of these people while there are still older generations praciticing the arts with a high level of skill. In the course of these expeditions, Henri has made lifelong friends among the Cree, who seem to appreciate his genuine interest as well as the sensitive and considerate manner in which he carries out his research.

Vaillancourt has built about a hundred canoes, yet he still hasn't gotten around to building a shop. The canoes take shape on a small rectangle of lawn sandwiched between the steep highway embankment and the houses of his mother and himself. An open shed, built off the rear quarter of his mother's house, provides some shelter from the rain. If things get really nasty, Henri will bring a canoe into his living room, where he can continue whatever step he'd started outside. Birch canoe building has always been a summer, or least a warm weather activity, and that is how it remains at Henri's.

Henri is 35, a handsome, surprisingly up-to-date looking man, who keeps fit through daily bicycling or snowshoeing. Year round he wears blue jeans and a plaid shirt, and you'll never catch him, even in the winter, in wool pants or the other accoutrements associated with the North. Although he can be dead serious about things like his canoe building and his research, his pervasive sense of humor is recurrently surfacing in any conversation; if he catches you with a ludicrous statement jammed in between the facts, he'll betray his mischief with a beaming boyish grin that lets you know you've been had. He has a passion for books — chiefly northwoods or historical in content — and the many loaded bookshelves built into his Bavarian-style home attest to his weakness.

Henri will tell you that the birchbark canoe at the zenith of its development in the 19th century was a refined, functional, and beautiful watercraft reflecting the ingenuity, woodscraft, and artistic expression of a resourceful people acquired over thousands of years. The white cedar planking and framing formed a marvelously flexible hull, which was protected and waterproofed by an incredibly durable skin, all lashed together by split spruce root into a form designed to maximize utility, while still pleasing the eye. Not every Indian in a village would build canoes, and the craftsmen within each tribe developed a definite style which was handed down through the generations. Little refinements by certain individuals of long ago can still be recognized by Henri's practiced eye.

According to Vaillancourt, the very finest canoes were built by the eastern Abenaki Indians, principally craftsmen of the Malecite, Passamaquoddy, and Penobscot tribes. The farther west one researches, the less likely one is to find this consistent quality, though this is not to say there were no skilled craftsmen among such tribes as the Ojibway and Algonquin. The Cree of the Romaine region of

Henri Vaillancourt, outside his Bavarian-style home.

Henri's canoes take shape in the yard outside his residence in Greenville, New Hampshire.

Québec were the equals of the Abenaki in the basic construction of their canoes, even though the materials available to them were far inferior — a testimony to superior craftsmanship which Henri can readily admire. But he points out the northern canoes lacked the artistic details which made the Abenaki canoes so remarkable.

Tools and Materials

The tools of a birchbark canoe builder are few and simple, and all the materials are available growing in most forests of the boreal regions of North America — although today truly fine materials are seldom found all in one small area. Because he is particular, Henri Vaillancourt ranges a fair distance for his own materials. Quality birchbark in quantities sufficient for his needs can be found in his own Granite State. His definition of quality gets more precise each year. It has come to mean a single sleeve of bark ⅛" in thickness, free of blemishes, long and wide enough to contain a 15' canoe without the addition of panels sewn onto the sides to accommodate the girth. It is a tall order to fill, and requires the careful felling (with a chainsaw these days) of a tree with a straight 24" trunk diameter, free of branches for about 20'. Once the tree is down, Henri slits the skin with a knife and using a square of thick bark with a chisel edge cut into it, removes the bark in one piece. He gathers his bark in June or July when the bark peels the easiest; so easily in fact, that it ofen takes no more than five minutes to slip the bark from the trunk, and one hour would be an uncommonly long struggle even with a difficult tree.

Once removed, the bark is rolled up, inside out (for that, of course, is how it will go on the canoe), and carried out. It may be stored indefinitely before being used. The best bark comes from Maine, Vermont, New Hampshire, the Maritimes, Québec, and eastern Ontario, but suitable birches grow west as far as Minnesota.

Henri has been cutting his white cedar in Maine, because he has access to a good supply that is convenient to get at, while he visits friends. The trees he takes vary from 12" to 18" in diameter, and just as with the birch, he looks for straight trees without twists, free of knots. When he uses cedar for the gunwales, he may split out sections up to 20' in length, but since the planking in a Vaillancourt canoe is butted amidships, 10' sections are all he normally needs for this use. The ribs, rarely more than 4' long, can be split from short butt ends of otherwise unsuitable logs. With the cedar down and cut to length, Henri inserts wooden wedges into a line of notches he has made the length of the log with his axe. From experience, he has a pretty good idea where this initial split should be started. He is usually right, and a few good whacks on the wedges in series normally lays the log open into two roughly symmetrical halves. These are split once or sometimes twice more, then the heartwood is removed from the sections. Normally further splitting of these sections takes place back in Greenville, but Vaillancourt frequently splits out the rib stock into rough frames right in the woods, resulting in less bulk to carry out and home. The froe splits the cedar roughly along the growth rings, and the resulting ribs have perfectly flat grain. When spruce (the choice among Indian builders north of the white cedar belt) is substituted, the sections are actually split across the growth rings, resulting in vertical-grain or "quarter-sawn" planking and ribs. Cedar may be split in this manner as well, but traditionally it was not and Henri sees no advantage to the method. He avoids the active sapwood just beneath the bark, because even in the white cedar, this young wood is prone to decay.

Parts of a birchbark.

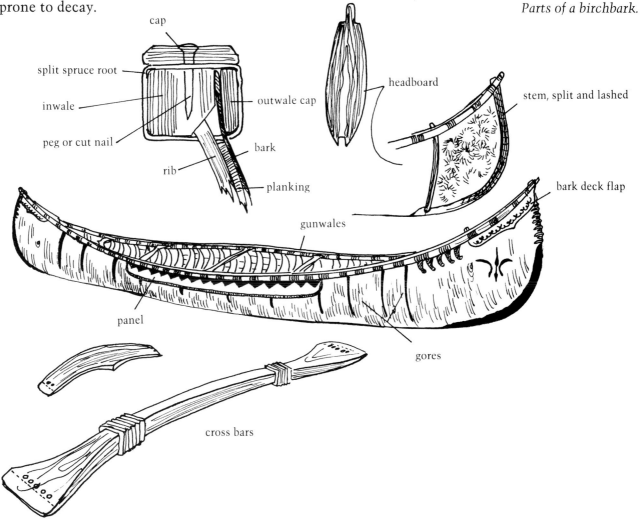

cap

split spruce root

inwale

peg or cut nail

rib

outwale cap

bark

planking

headboard

stem, split and lashed

bark deck flap

gunwales

gores

panel

cross bars

Henri likes the extra strength provided by spruce gunwales, but finds the spruce less willing than cedar to take the sharp upward bends at the ends of some of his models. Therefore, he takes the best tree of either species he happens to find while getting his rib and plank stock.

The other material gathered directly from the forest is spruce root, which is used in the critical lashing and sewing processes. Henri prefers root from the black or red spruces, but admits jack pine and red pine, as well as white spruce root are acceptable. The roots grow just beneath the forest floor, and he delights in finding a spruce grove with sphagnum moss carpeting beneath, because the roots are easy to pull and grow unobstructed into long straight lengths ideal for splitting. Typically the root Henri digs is ¼" in diameter and is immediately stripped of its skin. It is then rolled up and taken home for splitting, and may be stored for long periods before using so long as it is first soaked in water.

Back home, Henri finishes splitting out the cedar planking using first the froe, then a knife, peeling off ¼"-thick strips, which he dresses with his crooked knife until they are nearly as smooth and uniform as finished lumber from the mill. The Indians used crooked knives of bone, switching to iron and steel as soon as these materials become available. Some knives do indeed have a curved or a hooked blade, but most have a short, straight blade and the name crooked knife derives from the distinctively "bent" handle. To use the knife, the builder holds the stock to be worked against the body trunk, grasps the crooked knife in an underhand grip with the thumb extended along the handle with the other hand, and draws it into the work toward his body in long even strokes. Wood may be removed very quickly in this manner, but there is enough control so that very light, even shaving may also be accomplished. Henri can use his knife to turn out a beautifully carved paddle or a thwart in a surprisingly short space of time. He makes his own blades from file steel and has at least two knives handy all the time, each ground differently for heavy and light shaving.

The 40 or so ribs that will go into the canoe are similarly dressed to ⅜" in thickness, 3-½" wide in the middle tapering to aout 2-½" at each end. In the canoe the wide ribs form an almost solid floor over the planking, offering a clean appearance, increased durability, and a fairer hull. Wide ribs were traditional in many Indian canoes, and Henri feels their advantages far outweigh the drawbacks.

Bent like a mantis over its prey, Henri deftly splits the root into two identical half-oval strands which part beneath his fingers and coil off to the sides. By carefully

The crooked knife, named for its grip, is an important tool to a traditional birchbark builder.

bending the whole root just beyond the split, he can influence the rift — keeping it from wandering off to one side and shearing off. The larger root may have to be split a second time to produce a strand with the fineness he requires for his sewing.

The 1-¼″ inwales are prepared green — squared and smoothed, the ends tapered in width and depth, and a chamfer cut along the bottom inside corner to receive the beveled tops of the ribs. Next, they are lashed temporarily to crosspieces which hold them opposed to one another exactly as they will be in the canoe. From above you can see the plan view, showing exactly how wide the beam will be and how quickly the width will diminish toward the stems. The vertical rise of the sheerline at the ends is achieved by weighting the center of this structure on the ground, and in stages bending the ends of the gunwales upwards and propping them up. Saturating the green wood with water helps keep stubborn wood from breaking during this process, which might take a week or more on more pronounced sheerlines. Once properly bent, the gunwales are left on their crude form to cure, until their tendency to straighten back out diminishes.

Vaillancourt uses the crooked knife to dress the split cedar ribs.

The gunwale frame for a future canoe (on horses) alongside a finished 15′ Malecite.

There were great variations in the profiles of the stems of bark canoes regionally. From right to left: Malecite, Passama-quoddy, Algonkin, Ojibway, Mic Mac, Cree-crookedcanoe, Algonkin style fur-trace canoe.

On canoes with extremely high tight curves at the bow, such as those of the Ojibway and Algonquin, even this tedious process is inadequate to safely form the gunwales into the proper configuration. To achieve these abrupt curves, the builder must actually split the ends of the gunwales into several layers or laminates, which are then easily bent and lashed in place.

Once it has cured, the gunwale framework is completed by replacing the temporary crosspieces with the permanent thwarts. The thwarts are carved from birch or ash with the crooked knife. In a Vaillancourt canoe, as in the finer Indian examples, they can be pieces of sculpture in themselves. Although flat along the bottom surface, the top of the thwart is carved into a gentle camber, the depth diminishing from about 3/4" in the center to just over half that thickness at the tenon on the ends. In plan view the thwarts are wide in the center, narrow considerable in the quarters, then flare out again to their greatest width at the very ends. This graceful curve is highlighted by a traditional square decoration at the thwart's narrowest point. Mortises are cut into the inwales, wooden pegs driven

The crossbars (thwarts) of a bark canoe are thinned and flared at the ends, then mortised and lashed into the inwales.

through the joint, and the whole lashed neatly together with the spruce root.

The Building Frame

White men building canoes for the fur trade brigades employed wooden platforms or beds on which the bark was layed out and the building begun. Vaillancourt sticks to the Indian method of building the canoes right on the ground. He does, however, use a building frame in addition to the gunwale structure, a flat representation of the shape of the bottom of the canoe, around which the bark is bent up to form the sides. The building form is in two sections to facilitate its removal once the gunwales and thwarts are installed.

Construction Begins

After cleaning and scraping the bark smooth, Henri rolls it out on the ground. The building frame is placed on the sheet to maximize the best portions of the bark, and then weighted down. The bark is softened with water and the edges are folded up to form the sides, held in place by stakes driven into the ground along the perimeter of the shape.

If the bark isn't wide enough to reach the proposed gunwales amidships, Henri will neatly sew in panels on each side to symmetrically achieve the desired girth. Because of the complex curves of the canoe — especially one in which the sides "tumblehome" — vertical wedges or "gores" must be cut along the sheerline to prevent the bark from bulging as the canoe takes shape. Once the gore is cut out, the V is closed and sewn shut. Henri seals all the seams from the

A decorated panel sewn into the topsides of a Vaillancourt birch bark.

inside as well as the outside. He prefers a mixture made from rosin, grease, and linseed oil to either natural pitch or a substitute he used on his earlier canoes which consisted of roofing tar and kerosene. The rosin-based sealer has been around at least since Thoreau traveled the Maine woods with his Penobscot Indian guide, Joe Polis, making it traditional enough to suit Henri. It is also very effective, goes on neatly when properly heated, and over time, shrinks unobtrusively into the lashed seams.

The gunwale-thwart structure is next lashed into place, along with the small outside gunwale or cap which is about 1-⅜" wide, chamfered along the bottom outside edge. To accomplish the lashing, Henri pierces the bark with an awl and neatly winds several turns of root around the gunwales and bark with just enough space between lashings to accommodate the tops of the ribs.

Vaillancourt makes the stems from cedar — splitting a 1"-square length into several laminations for three quarters of its length, bending them to the desired shape and lashing them together. The Malecite models Henri prefers display a simple but handsome profile, with the prow somewhat undercut and the moderate curve flared forward at the sheer. The top of the stem is visible between the protruding inwales, and the unsplit butt of the stem ends at the first rib. The stem is installed, and the ends of the canoe are sewn up before the ribs and planking are put in.

The ¼" planking in a Vaillancourt canoe varies from 4" to 1-½" in width. Each plank is tapered toward the ends, offering a neat, orderly pattern of lines on the inside. Henri squares the ends and butts them flush beneath the center rib, rather than shaping the butts to a point and overlapping them, which is another popular method. The planking along the bottom is neatly laid into place before the ribs are installed, but the topside planks can be fitted only after there are enough ribs in place to hold them tightly against the bark.

Bending a set of satisfactory ribs for a birchbark canoe takes a practiced eye and great skill. There are no forms or jigs to assure consistency, and the final results are largely dependent upon the builder's ability to derive accurate compound curves mentally, simply by looking at the wall-sided bark shape on the ground before him, and his dexterity in duplicating these images in the frames he is bending. During the process the hard-chined birchbark box must be transformed into a rounded, fair watercraft by the addition of these formed arches, and no one accomplishes this more carefully or with better results than Vaillancourt.

Henri uses a copper boiler to boil up the ribs, and when they are sufficiently supple removes them in pairs. Using either his foot or his knee as a fulcrum, he holds the ribs by both ends and carefully bends the wood to resemble what he projects to be a cross section of the canoe. The ends are then tied together, and five more ribs of decreasing girth are bent in the same manner and nested inside the first, forming a bundle of six bent ribs. It takes seven or more of these bundles to frame out a canoe, and to assure symmetry, each succeeding rib from a bundle will be placed in the opposite end of the canoe. It is the careful fitting of these ribs, sprung under tension with the ends held beneath the gunwales, that not only holds the planking in place, but also fills out the bark to a smooth configuration.

The ribs are allowed to cure in their bundles for up to a day before they are placed in the canoe. Once a rib is cut to its exact length, and a bevel cut along the two top edges, Henri puts it into the canoe, tilting it slightly until the ends fit into the chamfer on the underside of gunwale. Then, using a wooden maul and hammer, he drives the rib into its permanent position. He completes planking up the sides (all the way to the sheer) once there are enough ribs in place to sufficiently hold the planking in place against the bark. Then, one by one, all the ribs are installed to his satisfaction. Frequently a rib that doesn't fit closely enough is removed for further soaking and rebending. This truing up and adjustment of the frames can be very time consuming, but Vaillancourt says it is absolutely necessary to achieve the fair hulls and taut bark skin which are among the trademarks of his work.

Final Details

At this time, the canoe may be turned over and the outside of the seams treated with pitch. The decks on a birch canoe are pieces of bark bent over the ends which are sandwiched between the inner and outer gunwales, the edges protruding from beneath the outwales a couple of inches. This flap is cut in an attractive pattern, and Henri further decorates the overlap with "winterbark work" — a type of etching process in which the thin, tough, brownish skin of the very inside of a bark is scraped away in a manner that forms a contrasting pattern or design against the lighter layer beneath.

The headboard — a small bulkhead arrangement near each end — is carved from cedar and notched to fit into the butt of the stem at the bottom and between the gunwales at the sheer. In profile, the headboard is slightly arched toward the stem. The space ahead of the headboard is filled with moss to help the bow keeps its shape — especially critical in canoes with tumblehome in the ends.

Henri Vaillancourt hefting a finished canoe by one of its gracefully carved crossbars.

A ¼"-thick cap piece wide enough to cover both inside and outside gunwales and the lashings is then installed along the sheerline with wooden pegs or sqaure-cut nails. Henri says that the cap not only gives the canoe a finished appearance, but also protects the lashings and adds rigidity to the sheerline. It prevents the gunwales from relaxing between the thwarts in subsequent years — forming hard spots at each crosspiece.

Henri has never painted the interior of one of his canoes, but in the 19th century it was not an uncommon practice, and he wouldn't mind doing it if it were requested by a customer. Naturally, most bark canoe aficionados relish the rich, natural appearance of wood itself. He does lay on a coat of oil and turpentine, which accentuates the tone and highlights the contours in the new canoe as well as affords some protection. The bow of the canoe is often decorated with a painted fleur-de-lis or other appropriate symbol, and simple designs are sometimes painted in Indian fashion on the panels sewn in along the sheer.

Ensuring the Bark Canoe's Survival

It is difficult not to believe in pre-destination after talking to Henri about his career. How else would you explain a five-year-old boy in Greenville, New Hampshire, in the 1950s stripping bark from a pine tree, and sewing the panels together with needle and thread. At age 14, armed with an illustrated edition of *Hiawatha*, and an article from *Sports Afield*, he launched his second attempt, which resulted in a crude but completed Ojibway-style canoe. Young Vaillancourt gathered and sewed together the bark skin for the canoe and roughed out the gunwales from hemlock saplings, then built the canoe using hemlock ribs sawn out by his father, and planking cut from 2x4s.

An older friend, admiring Henri's efforts, presented him with a copy of Adney and Chapelle's *The Bark Canoes and Skin Boats of North America*, and thus inspired and informed, he went about building what he terms "an essentially good canoe" at age 18, using sawn rather than split cedar for ribs and planking.

Vaillancourt's career at the University of New Hampshire forestry school in the late '60s was not a long or particularly enlightening affair. He discovered right off that most of the jobs that would be open to him upon graduation would be with large corporate landowners on their managed timberlands — not the romantic possibilities of which he had dreamed. The administration allowed him to complete his freshman year taking coures that interested him personally — anthropology and philosophy mostly, so long as he agreed not to return the following year.

Faced with the prospects of working at one of the mills or for a building contractor, he set about building a bark canoe — a 14' Abenaki, which he sold to a collector in 1971. By the end of the following year he was selling all he could make, and he has been booked ahead for years ever since. Although in the mid-'70s he would build up to eight canoes a year, today, in the interest of producing better quality canoes (most people would call them perfect) and allowing more time for his research, he builds just three canoes each year. He has begun charging prices that justify the more than 400 hours and careful attention that go into each canoe — but no one is complaining about prices that run about $300 per foot.

In 1973, author and *New Yorker* columnist John McPhee paid Henri a visit and based upon subsequent interviews and a trip through Thoreau's Maine with Vaillancourt and a friend, wrote a series of articles for the magazine that found their way into the popular book *The Survival of the Birch Bark Canoe*. It is obvious to the reader of *Survival* that the two personalities did not exactly mesh, and that Henri's woodscraft on the trip did not meet McPhee's expectations. Vaillancourt was not informed in advance that the articles were being made into a book, and as an unfortunate result the two have not since spoken. Nonetheless, many people have been introduced to Henri and his work through the book, which has considerable information on the canoes and birchbark building.

In Henri's view, a much more positive occurrence that same year was his first trip to the Indian reserve at Mistassini, where he was introduced to many of the excellent

Vaillancourt carefully lashes the top of the stem to the bark with finely split spruce root.

Superior materials, impeccable craftsmanship, and artistic details are all trademarks of a Vaillancourt canoe.

traditional crafts that were being carried on there, and to the families who were practicing them. In 1977, the Trust for American Cultures and Crafts was founded by Henri and partner and video technician, Todd Crocker. Using a borrowed, professional-quality video camera, they produced a number of excellent tapes on such subjects as snowshoe, toboggan, and canoe building, and eventually purchased the unit with their own money — a considerable investment in the early days of technology. Today Henri's interests in northern cultures ranges globally, and it is his hope that through the Trust, he will be able to preserve on tape and in books the material cultures of northern-dwelling people throughout the world. He feels pressured to obtain as much information as soon as possible before it fades forever from the face of the changing world. Currently he is putting the finishing touches on a beautifully illustrated book detailing the building of the Attitamek snowshoe. Wherever his work has taken him, Henri has built lasting friendships with his subjects, and each year he makes an effort to stay in touch with the people he has gotten to know through his research in the distant north.

It is hard to figure out a fellow who builds lovely and functional birch canoes, is an accomplished paddler in the Indian style, but has minimal interest in canoe travel recreationally; or a man who since childhood has focused his attention on the fading cultures of traditional American Indians, yet recognizes practically at the birth of the technology, the important role video recording can play in preserving these cultures. But explanations aside, Henri's work is unique and important, and his bark canoes are priceless heirlooms that reflect the best refinements of an amazing traditonal technology that has provided the basis for all subsequent modern canoe building.

A Brief History of the Wood & Canvas Canoe

2

During the 1870s around the lumbering capital of the world, Bangor, Maine, the wood and canvas canoe was developed based on the local Penobscot Indian birchbark canoe. The construction principles of the wood-canvas canoe were similar to those of the bark canoe in that there were wide, thin, flexible ribs and planking covered with a strong waterproof covering, independent of the wooden hull, with strong rails and thwarts to help maintain the canoe's shape and strength. The actual construction of the wood-canvas canoe, however, is the reverse of that of a bark canoe. The use of a solid form starting with the ribs and planking and applying the outside covering last is opposite to the Indian building method.

An Uncivilized Craft?

The wood-canvas canoe was completely different from any other craft at that time, and it may be assumed that a review of sporting newspapers, books, and articles of that period would reveal its development from the bark canoe. But a review of those documents reveals that the indigenous bark canoe was not considered worthy of attenion by the period media, and any craft that based its construction and use upon it was also considered to be inferior and unworthy of civilized society. Perhaps the best known and largest newspaper of that time that reported on canoeing, hunting, and other sporting news was *Forest and Stream*. A query in 1874 to *Forest and Stream* requesting information on bark canoes was answered with: "We are reluctant to inform our anxious inquirer that the birchbark canoe is not named or known in the category of civilized craft which our modern canoeman paddle and sail....It is the peculiar toy and vehicle of the aboriginal redskin and although it is light and buoyant and full of poetry and well adapted to his requirements, the palefaces are conceited enough to believe that they can manufacture something better in all respects."

Miniature Yachts

In 1880 the American Canoe Association was formed and began regular canoeing reports through various publications. The type of canoe the A.C.A. emphasized was the all-wood, decked-over sailing canoe. This type of canoe traced its history back to 1865 when a Scotsman, John MacGregor, wrote an immediately popular book, *A Thousand Miles in the Rob Roy*, based on his European tour in a lapstrake-style canoe. The all-wood hull of this type of canoe was made watertight by each plank lapping over the plank below it with a series of fastenings to keep it tight. Mr. Baden-Powell modified MacGregor's Rob Roy for better sailing qualities and called his canoe the Nautilus. This type of sailing canoe became very popular at the New York Canoe Club, which formed the nucleus of the A.C.A. The canoes of the A.C.A. were mostly decked like a kayak, had two or more sails, yet were normally under 16' long. They would have centerboards and keels for sailing, and when paddled a double-bladed paddle was used. Looking much like miniature yachts, they were built using European technology.

Canadian Developments

"The American Travelling" canoe built by J.H Rushton, 1882, modeled after MacGregor's "Rob Roy."

Since the 1860s the Canadians around Peterborough, Ontario, had been developing an all-wood canoe based on dug-outs in their region. The Peterborough canoes were

New York State Historical Association

built using European boatbuilding techniques; however, their canoes were not decked over, could carry two or more people, were propelled by a single-bladed paddle, and could be sailed as well as paddled on streams and rivers. The A.C.A. looked down on these fine craft because they did not perform as well as the American sailing canoes. As late as 1890, the A.C.A. reported "Canoeing in the States is essentially different from that in Canada. About the great cities, the center of canoeing, the waters are broad and best fitted for sailing; there is little field for gunning and hunting and no need to use the canoe for this purpose, while canoeists as a rule have less leisure for extended trips than their Canadian cousins...." The versatile open Canadian canoe, however, still proved very popular and the A.C.A. finally did accept them as a class of canoe, especially after they started defeating the Americans at the A.C.A. meets.

The Maine Canoe

Journals and organizations of the period promoted canoeing as a sport for gentlemen and the elite. They liked to think they had nothing in common with the class of people who used the canoe as a tool — the Indian, the professional

Branden Powell's sailing canoe "Nautilus" at the American Canoeing Association 1886 Meet.

New York State Historical Association

guide, and the woodsman. From time to time the wood-canvas canoe was brought to their attention, but each time is was successfully ignored. In 1876 *Forest and Stream* gave the first printed report of a revolutionary style of canoe. "A person from Nova Scotia reports a previously unknown canoe style that was brought to Yarmouth by a Joseph Johnson from Bangor, Maine: "I can not say exactly how constructed, but I think that the gunwale is made first to which ribs of pine, about 2" wide and ⅛" thick, are bent to the form desired. Longitudinal strips of the same are tacked as closely as possible to the ribs outside, and over all a covering of canvas is tightly stretched...." The established canoeing world remained uninterested in what they termed "Rag" canoes except for portable canvas canoes that had a collapsible frame.

But in 1910, when wood-canvas canoes were flooding the market, suddenly *Forest and Stream* and the A.C.A. were wondering where they had come from. They generally concluded the canvas canoe had been developed around 1900 around Old Town, Maine, even though the outstanding company of B.N. Morris of Veazie, Maine, had advertised it in their magazine in the 1890s. The A.C.A. did not accept the wood-canvas canoe as a class until 1934, even though it had been the most popular canoe in the recreation field for almost 30 years. They continued to class all open canoes as "Canadian"-style canoes, even though the American canvas canoes had little in common with the all-wood Peterboroughs. The evolution of the wood-canvas canoe went unnoticed by the established canoeing world and largely unreported or advertised by the local publications or the builders themselves.

In Maine, the birchbark canoe was the only type of canoe in use. The bark canoe was in great demand among the communities along the Penobscot River, and the individual Indian builders were not able to meet the demand. In

Maine wilderness travel by bark canoe and batteau. The Fredrick Church expedition on the Penobscot River West Branch at Katepsconegan Carry, 1874.

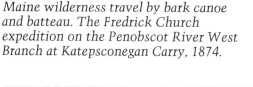

Stoddar Collection, Maine State Library

Old Town, Maine, Guy Carleton had a good business building batteaux and bark canoes for the lumbermen. The little town of Lowell, just up river from Old Town, produced two of the better non-native bark builders, J. Darling and Bill McLain. Both Darling and McLain had bark canoe factories, and during the 1870s Bill McLain and his son produced over 75 canoes a year, many of them going to the Bar Harbor Canoe Club.

By the late 1870s, the bark builders were having difficulty obtaining bark and were having to import it from considerable distances; the use of canvas as a substitute for bark was becoming more common. In 1885 the Bangor paper *The Industrial Journal* reported: "About 10 years ago canvas began to be used in place of bark as a covering for canoes and a great many of this description are now made in Bangor. They are covered with a thick coat of paint to make them watertight and are lighter and fully as cheap ($35) but not as symmetrical as a birch. The duck (canvas) cost $6 for an ordinary 18′ canoe." The article goes on to predict "Bark will never be driven out by canvas, for it bends prettier and is a more romantic material than duck."

The use of canvas as a substitute for bark, or even as a covering over a leaky bark canoe, was not a new idea. For many years before the 1880s, various Indian builders,

Typical Maine bark canoe in 1876 on the West Branch of the Penobscot River in the shadow of Mount Katahdin.

Stoddar Collection, Maine State Library

woodsmen, and even the Hudson's Bay Company of Canada had canoes built by this method and it is still used today by Indians in the Romaine region of Québec where birchbark has never been available. Essentially, this method is a variation of existing birchbark technology and does not appear to be a forerunner of the canvas-covered canoe built over a solid form.

Building on a Form

Guides and sport in early wood & canvas canoes in the 1880s, similar in design to the Penobscot bark canoes.

It was not until the builders of Maine completely changed the building system that the wood-canvas canoe came into its own. The theory of building upside down, over a form with metal straps, nailing the ribs and planking together and stretching the canvas over the wood hull must have been a radical idea to the Maine builders. The builders of the all-wood American sailing canoes and the Peterborough canoes had been using canoe forms since the 1860s, and it would seem reasonable that those building

Stoddar Collection, Maine State Library

methods would eventually be copied by the Maine builders. However, there is no indication that the Maine builders were aware of the other building techniques. The all-wood canoes were not in use in the woods of Maine, and there were no builders using these techniques in the region. The early Maine builders were woodsmen and guides, self-taught craftsmen with little formal education, who had neither the time nor the money to travel or engage in the leisure activity of recreational canoeing. The builders in Peterborough developed a form for their type of canoe, and it is not unreasonable to assume that the Maine builders did the same for their own canoes in the late 1870s.

The use of the form enabled the builder to do many things that couldn't be done with the bark canoes. It guaranteed the shape of the canoe and produced a stronger canoe because of the mechanical fastenings and uniform size of the material. The parts could be mass produced with less skilled labor. By keeping the traditional parts and shape of the bark canoe — the thin planking braced with thicker ribs spaced every 3″ or 4″, the hull sheathed with a strong, independent flexible waterproof covering — the canoe retained the resilience and responsiveness and overall shape of the original bark canoe.

Why the Maine builders never published more about this development is a mystery; we can only speculate. First, the development of the form may have been perfected over a short period of time by several different men, improving on each others' ideas, each one feeling the idea was a commonly known one. Second, the early builders were all used to labor as woodsmen or guides, and had very little formal education; in the tradition of the tight-lipped Yankee, they were not very good at self-promotion and felt their craftsmanship spoke for itself. In the early catalogs they all seem to claim some credit for the advancement of the wood-canvas canoe, but no one would come right out and say that he was responsible for its development, as evidenced by the following excerpts:

1898, E.H. Gerrish, Bangor, Maine: Twenty years experience has given the inventor the only perfect filler for making canoes perfectly waterproof.

1922, G.E. Carleton, Old Town, Maine: The Carleton model canvas-covered canoe is a reproduction from a birchbark canoe belonging to the Penobscot or Tarratine tribe of Indians. It has been on the market for more than 30 years, being the pioneer in the modern canoe.

1901, B.N. Morris, Veazie, Maine: I wish to impress that this style of construction is not a new idea, but one which has been in practical use at least 25 years, and has proven a perfect success....It was first built in a very rough manner but its use has been so largely taken up and many being desirous of a fine canoe of that style, the construction has been improved upon (in which I have a claim for considerable credit).

1910, E.M. White, Old Town, Maine: The White canoe, pioneer in such craft, is among the earliest descendants of the birch.

Early Maine Builders

The earliest commercial builder of wood-canvas canoes appears to be Evan(Eve) H. Gerrish of Bangor, Maine. Gerrish was a hunting and fishing guide from Brownville, Maine, who came to Bangor in 1875 and started a small one-man business manufacturing fishing rods and canoe paddles but also started experiments with a wood-canvas building system. According the the Gerrish family history as told by Eve's grandnephew, Henry Gerrish of Dover-Foxcroft, Maine, Eve was quite exasperated with the leaky bark canoes that he had to use as a woods guide. While on a trip to Onawa Lake, Eve experimented with using canvas on a bark canoe. No one remembers exactly how or why Gerrish was able to stop guiding, move to Bangor at the age of 28, and purchase a shop in the heart of the business area of Bangor. According to Henry Gerrish, there is an unauthenticaed family story that while Eve was guiding a "sport" on Moosehead Lake, the sport became involved in a life-threatening situation; Eve was able to rescue the client and was rewarded with a substantial sum, which afforded Eve some financial freedom. There is no way to verify this story. In 1942, however, Mr. Harold Hinckley was interviewed by the *Bangor Daily Commercial* and it reported: "His father, Frank Hinckley of Broadway Street, assisted Mr. Evan Gerrish financially and otherwise in the first enterprise for revolutionizing canoes. Mr. Hinckley states that the first canoe built of canvas did not prove as satisfactory as desired, so a second experiment was tried and that proved to be a success. From that time on canvas canoes were improved upon as occurred to inventive minds." Why Frank Hinckley, whose family had a very large and successful ironworks business in Bangor, would become involved in a one-man shop with a guide from Brownville is not explained, but it does add credibility to the Gerrish family story.

Regardless of how it evolved, by 1878 Gerrish was regularly producing about 18 canoes a year at his shop at 18 Broad Street. By 1882 he had hired his first employee and was building about 25 canoes a year at the average price of $25 each. The reputation of the canvas canoe was spreading to the recreational market. Gerrish already had customers far from Maine, and in 1884 he was producing over 50 canoes annually and had sent several canoes to an exhibit at the New Orleans Exposition.

Soon other companies up river from Bangor were developing their own canvas canoes and improving the manufacturing process. B.N. Morris started the Veazie Boat and Canoe Company on the second floor of his home in Veazie in 1882. It soon became the B.N. Morris Canoe Company, and for a long time it was one of the largest and best known canoe companies in the world until a fire destroyed the factory in 1920. Up river from Veazie, at Gilman Falls, E.M. White started producing canoes in 1888. In an interview in 1901 in the *Old Town Enterprise,* Mr. White told how he became interested in building canvas canoes. "I saw a man by the name of Evan Gerrish of Bangor riding in the Penobscot River in a canvas-covered canoe. I quickly saw the advantages of that kind over my birchbark, which moreover leaked. I examined the canvas canoe closely, and in a short time was able to produce one which was so good someone wanted to buy it." White started building canoes at his Gilman Falls family home by boiling ribs in his mother's washtub and using a horse on a treadmill for power. White's brother-in-law, E.L. Hinckley, became a working partner and provided the capital to open a large shop in nearby Old Town. The Carleton Boat and Canoe Company of Old Town built batteaux and bark canoes in the 1870s. Carleton appears to be the only one of the batteaux and/or bark builders who switched to building canvas canoes and as such was the only one who brought any previous boatbuilding experience to the industry. Carleton was later bought by the Old Town Canoe Company in the early 1920's.

The Canvas Canoe

The designs of the canvas canoe were copies of the bark canoe of the local Penobscot Indians. They were easy to paddle, narrow, shallow, and their sheerline has a low profile. Many people today would be uncomfortable in them, but they suited paddlers who had grown up using canoes. The construction of the early canvas canoes was much like the barks. The closed-gunwale system presented difficul-

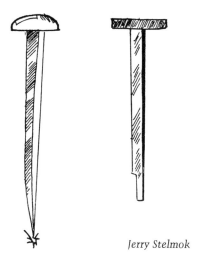

Jerry Stelmok

Old style bunt tack vs. the more modern sharp, oval headed tack.

ties, but the builders were already familiar with it. In the bark canoe there was a strong inwale with lashings around the rail to secure the bark to it. Thin top and outside caps protected the lashings. The canvas builders also used a strong inwale and tapered the ribs and planking to a feather edge at the top of the rail. The outside cap covered the ends of the ribs and the edge of the canvas. The top gave the rail system a finished appearance. Bark canoes did not have structural decks, only a flap of bark to protect the lashings that held the rails together at the ends of the canoe. The canvas builders inserted a small deck between the rails and used nails to hold the rails together along with the lashings. Well into the 1890s, many of the builders were still using symbolic lashings around the deck, perhaps because that is what people expected to see. Until around 1900 the majority of all decks had the same general heart shape.

At first, finely carved thwarts were mortised and lashed to the inwale just as on the barks. This was time consuming and it weakened the inwale. It wasn't long before stronger, heavier thwarts were bolted to the bottom of the inwale. The early canoe tacks were not tacks at all but cut copper nails. They were fairly blunt and wide by today's standards, but they would clinch reasonable well and would not corrode. The first real canoe tacks with a narrow body and fine tip were also of copper and became available in the 1890s.

The exterior canvas not only had to be made watertight, but the weave had to somehow be protected from the scrapes and abrasions that could quickly wear through it. It also had to be protected from mildew and rot and made smooth enough to be an effective base for an attractive finish paint, yet flexible enough so the movement of the canoe and the drying effect of the sun would not crack it. The early applications of linseed oil and layers of paint did not prove very durable, and it wasn't long before more

A typical Gerrish closed gunwale canoe with a narrow heart shape deck, a small hand carrying thwart and symbolic lashings around the tips of the rails.

complicated formulas were developed. E.H. Gerrish advertised quite extensively that he had invented the best canvas filler. Each company developed its own fillers and was very secretive about the exact formulas. The basic ingredients were boiled linseed oil, coloring, thinner, Japan dryer, white lead, and silica powder. Several applications were hand-rubbed into the canvas weave and allowed to dry for up to four weeks before being lightly sanded and painted. The majority of today's builders still use adaptations of the original formulas and still guard them as closely as the early builders did.

Canoe clubs along the Charles River and the Connecticut River in Massachusetts readily accepted the new canvas canoes. Hundreds of people took to the calm water on weekends — not to go anywhere in particular, but just to socialize. This was a totally new type of canoeing, for which the builders in Maine were not prepared. Some early canvas canoe builders designed their canoes for the Cha-

The Market Grows

1890s E.M. White canoe on Moosehead Lake near Kineo. Note the closed gunwales, carved thwarts that are mortised into the inwale, stern seat for the guide, and the bottom canoe seat for the sport.

C.T. Crosby "Fly Rod" Collection, Maine State Museum

rles River market — canoes with picturesque high bows, wide flat bottoms for good stability, and straight keels so they would paddle in a straight line easily. These canoes were characterized by fancy details including long, wide decks with coamings and thick, heavily shaped thwarts with two seats; the Maine canoes, if they had any seats at all, would only have one in the stern. J.R. Robertson of Auburndale, Massachusetts, was one of the very early such builders, beginning in the early 1880s. Canoe builders did very well with this recreational market, and managing canoe liveries and rentals became a major buisness along the Charles River.

As canoeing expanded to the general recreational public in the 1890s, safety became a big concern. Many people did not feel at home in a canoe, so the Maine companies started making their canoes wider and fuller, stressing their safety. A B.N. Morris advertisment stated: "Canoeing is Dangerous — under certain Conditions." E.M. White boasted: "Absolute safety in Canoes — well built, unsinkable." Of course any wood canoe by itself is unsinkable, but White enhanced this quality with the addition of sponsons to the sides of the canoe. During the early 1890s, watertight chambers were added to the outside of the canoe just below the rail. The sponson is a canvas-covered, strip-planked frame, about 4″ wide and 6″ deep at the center of the canoe, tapering to a feather edge at the ends of the canoe. They are essentially air tanks along the top edge of the canoe and they also make the canoe 8″ wider, making it nearly impossible to upset and providing excellent flotation even if the canoe is filled with water.

The recreational public embraced sponsons, and soon all the other companies had their own style. In 1908, C.B. Thatcher of Bangor was granted a patent for invisible sponsons. Thatcher built canoes in Bangor from 1890 to 1915;

Recreational canoeing along the Charles River was a serious social event in the late 1800s and early 1900s.

Wooden Canoe Heritage Association

Advertisement from the Maine
Sportsman, *1897.*

Sponson canoe from 1902 E.M. White catalog.

not much else in known about him except that he was almost the only American wood-canvas canoe builder who tried to patent part of the wood-canvas construction technology. The "invisible" sponsons were similar to the ordinary variety except that they were tapered farther down the side of the canoe so that they did not appear to bulge out on the sides. Thatcher did not have much luck keeping this style of sponson to himself. E.M. White had already been using them since 1906, and the Kennebec Canoe Co. of Waterville, Maine, later used the invisible sponson system, but almost no other company followed suit.

Old Town Canoe

A bit of advice, offered in the Old Town newspaper, *The Enterprise*, in December, 1894 proved prophetic: "A canoe factory would pay well in Old Town. One that would turn out a hundred or so a month. Don't let anyone make you believe that a sale of canoes cannot be created. There are hundreds of towns and cities in the U.S. with a lake or pond close by, and the canoe could be made popular in these places as the bicycle has been where good roads exist — and the luxury could be had for *less* money. It is small industries that will make the future of Old Town, and the canoe business will be one of them." There were already seven or more builders in Old Town: G.E. Carleton and E.M. White, who employed five or six men, as well as smaller companies such as Heart and Snow, Arthur Godrey, Louis Leavitt, Henry Wickett, and I. Ingalls. Altogether they produced about 300 canoes a year in the mid-1890s.

In 1900 the *Enterprise's* statement began to become a reality. An entrepreneur, George Gray, whose family operated many businesses in town, either bought Wickett's small company and/or hired Wickett to build canoes behind Gray's hardware store in Old Town. It is believed that Gray originally sold the canoes under the name of "Wickett Canoe." The canoe business progressed rapidly; George's brother, Herbert, invested in the company, and in 1901 the company was called the "Indian Old Town Canoe Company." Business outgrew the facilities of the hardware store and the wood-frame, four-story Keith Shoe factory was purchased for the canoe factory. Early in 1902, to obtain more building experience and perhaps to gain a stonger influence in the Charles River area and the recreational canoeing market, John R. Robertson of Auburndale, Massachusetts, was brought in as the company's superintendent. Robertson had almost 20 years' experience running a successful operation building and renting canoes in the Charles River area. A new corporation was formed with

Ruth Gray

George Gray, Founder of Old Town Canoe.

Old Town Canoe Company

J.R. Robertson, Superintendent of Robertson-Old Town Canoe 1902-04.

Old Town Canoe Company

In 1903 the former Keith Shoe factory became the home of Old Town Canoe.

Ruth Gray

Samuel Gray developed and managed Old Town Canoe from 1905 until 1961.

H. Gray, President; long-time Gray employee, George Richardson, Treasurer; and J.R. Robertson, Superintendent. The exact terms of Robertson's coming to Old Town are unclear, but he had to have had substantial influence in the firm because the company's name was changed to the Robertson-Old Town Canoe Company. But whatever Robertson's early influence in the company was, by 1904 nothing more was heard of him in connection with the company and the company's name was changed once again to the name that became world famous: the Old Town Canoe Company. The Robertson canoe company in Auburndale appears to have continued to build canoes during this period, and it continued on as a company until the 1940s. Louis Leavitt, another area builder, went to work for Old Town Canoe at about this time.

Old Town's first canoe models were the H.W. (reportedly for Henry Wickett) model and the I.F. model, which later became known as the guide model. The Robertson model was added in 1902. In 1904 that name was changed to the Charles River model. The famous Otca model was added in 1906. Although Old Town was to add many different styles and types of canoes and boats, these four canoe models were to serve as the core of production for the next 50 years.

In 1903 George Gray's son, Samuel, graduated from Bowdoin and in 1904 began to take over the management of the Old Town Canoe Company. Unlike the other canoe company proprietors at that time, the Grays were not canoe builders themselves and the company was not established with their designs. What they did bring to the industry were keen business skills and an entrepreneural spirit that far exceeded that of any other American canoe company. Their aggressive advertising, promoting the wood-canvas canoe's Indian heritage as based in Old Town, and the

Old Town Canoe Company

Old Town Canoe Company factory as it was developed in 1914 and as it stands today.

quality of their product accelerated Old Town's growth. By 1912 and 1914 major four- and five-story brick additions were added to the original building, enabling the company to build the hundreds of canoes a month that the *Enterprise* had predicted.

The great Canadian company, Chestnut Canoe, was established much as Old Town Canoe was. In 1897 the Chestnut brothers, William and Harry, noticed the new style of canoes coming into Fredericton, New Brunswick, from Maine by way of the St. John River. The brothers were heirs to the Chestnut Hardware Company, which had been established in Fredericton since 1832, and they were very well entrenched in the business community. William and Harry recognized the advantages of this new style of canoe, and noted that the duty made their import into Canada unprofitable, suggesting that they could be built there for a good profit. By 1899 the Chestnut Canoe Company had hired a local boatbuilder, Jack Moore, to reproduce the Maine canoes. The Chestnut Canoe Company grew rapidly and like Old Town Canoe, needed experienced builders in order to expand. In 1904 William Chestnut traveled to Old Town, Maine, to try to convince experienced builders to come to work for Chestnut. It is unknown what luck he had at the other canoe companies, but at Old Town he was able to convince 10 workmen to move to Fredericton and work for Chestnut. Old Town Canoe was upset over this situation, especially since it was reported that Mr. Chestnut

Chestnut Canoe

An early Chestnut canvas canoe and a Peterborough style strip canoe built by Walter Walker. Note the heart shaped deck on the Chestnut. The strip canoe has no exterior covering. The narrow strips of planking are rabbited for a tight fit and fastened to closely spaced, narrow ribs. No glue, caulking epoxy, or fiberglass!

Jeff Dean

went right into their factory to do some of his recruiting. A lawsuit was filed against Chestnut, but the outcome of the suit is not known. In 1905, however, the Chestnut Company greatly expanded its operation and added six more canoe models.

Chestnut was able to do something that no American company was able to do — it obtained a Canadian patent for "Wood and Canvas Canoe Construction Technique." Although the builders in Peterborough had been using roughly the same technique of using a form to build their all-wood canoes upside down for over 20 years, this patent would prevent them from building wood-canvas canoes. Chestnut won a lawsuit that defended its right to the patent and gave it momentum to become the largest producer of wooden canoes in Canada until the company closed in 1979.

Open-Gunwale Construction

It seems incredible in retrospect, but the development of the open-gunwale style of construction for the rails was not developed until around 1905. It is very difficult to drain the water from a closed-gunwale canoe. The capped rail always traps a certain amount of water even when the canoe is turned on its side. Moisture is always present, and it accelerates dry rot in the rails and the tops of the ribs. With open gunwales, the water is easy to drain, reducing the problem of dry rot. The larger outside rail also made a stronger rail system, and the ends of the ribs did not have to be tapered to a feather edge, so they were stronger also. The open-gunwale construction was easier and faster to build, and it did not require any major changes in the existing canoe forms. Nevertheless, it took a while for the builders to adapt to it, and all the builders charged $2 to $3 more for the open gunwales. In 1906 Old Town Canoe introduced

An early open gunwale canoe by E.H. Gerrish. There are small ½" wide caps on top of the inwale and outside rail, leaving the space between the ribs open so water could drain out.

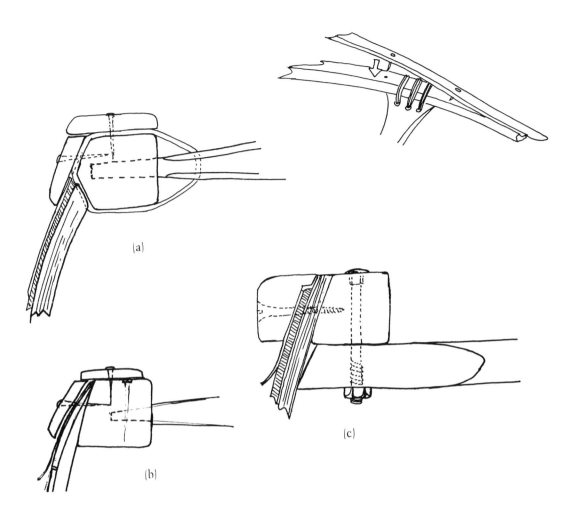

Gunwale styles: a) closed style on a bark canoe, b) closed style on an early canvas canoe, c) open gunwale style on the modern canvas canoe. Water can drain from between the ribs beacause there is no cap.

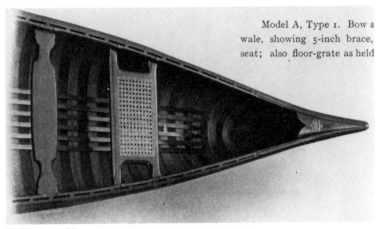

Model A, Type 1. Bow s
wale, showing 5-inch brace,
seat; also floor-grate as held

A 1905 open gunwale B.N. Morris canoe. Note the narrow inwale, heavy outwale and the traditional heart shape deck.

Maine State Museum

their "Ideal" canoe model, a Charles River model canoe with the "NEW" open gunwales. The B.N. Morris company made the system available on all of their models by 1910, but all the companies continued to show closed gunwales as standard construction in their catalogs until around 1918. After 15 years the public was finally convinced of the advantages, and the closed system was dropped completely from most catalogs in the early 1920s.

Motor Options

E.M. White was one of the first companies to place gasoline engines in its canoes, in the early 1890s. A one-horsepower Palmer engine was mounted inside the canoe, requiring a shaft that ran through the hull to a propeller. This inboard motor was not practical for regular canoes, however; larger motor canoes were developed to be used as launches and runabouts. Most companies offered a motor option, but only a few companies, including White and Gerrish, ever put them in their catalogs. White motor canoes were exceptionally well designed, with "invisible" sponsons and a molded, rounded deck edge to give the whole topside of the boat a graceful, curved appearance.

1902 E. M. White motor canoes with "Invisible" sponsons.

The two-horsepower Palmer jump-spark, two-cycle motors yielded a top speed of nine miles per hour, the four-horsepower gave 12 miles per hour.

The outboard motor, developed by Evinrude and Johnson, was becoming fairly dependable by the early 1920s. By using a motor mount attached to the side of the canoe, the removable motor extended the use of any canoe. The inboard-motor canoe faded as the outboard became more popular, and the square-stern canoe was designed to take advantage of the outboard motor. The square-stern canoe placed the motor on the centerline of the boat instead of off to one side as with a side motor mount, and it provided a rugged transom on which to mount the motor. The stern was wider than the stern of a normal canoe to provide more flotation for the motor and operator. Paddling qualities of the square sterns were not very good because at low speeds, a square, flat stern creates more drag in the water than that produced by a symmetrical hull.

The fitting of motors at the B.N. Morris factory, 1914.

Maine State Museum

The Grand Laker

Even with a motor, the guides of Grand Lake Stream, Maine, found that they still did a lot of paddling and poling guiding their sports to the fishing areas around West Grand Lake. Canoe builder and woodsman Herbert (Beaver) Bacon is generally credited with developing what became known as the Grand Lake Stream Canoe — or simply the Grand Laker — around 1924. Other area builders such as Joe Sprague (who learned bark canoe building from the celebrated Indian, Joe Mell) and Arthur Wheaton and his father-in-law, Dr. Whiting, also develped square-stern Grand Lakers at about the same time. By introducing a small transom and curving the last 3′ of these large 20′ canoes up to meet the transom, they kept the bottom profile of the canoe more like that of a symmetrical hull. The motors were generally under five horsepower, relatively light, which meant the canoes responded to paddling and poling as well as motoring. Over the years the transoms have become wider and deeper to accommodate the more powerful and dependable motors.

The proud, independent builders of Grand Lake Stream never developed a single, strong canoe company and each builder remained independent and tended to use canoe building to supplement his income as a guide or woodsman. Together they were a substantial canoe-building force in Maine and New Brunswick. Today, Grand Lake Stream is perhaps the last area in the United States where there is an active community of wooden canoe builders who learned their craft from their fathers and grandfathers.

A model canoe built by "Beaver" Bacon in 1923 to help design his Grand Lake Stream motor canoe.

Tim Bacon working on another Grand Lake Stream canoe from the same form his father developed in the early 1920s.

The Zenith, and Then....

By the late 1920s the wood and canvas canoe had evolved into its present style and construction. The canoe's era reached its zenith in the 1920s due to the popularity of canoe clubs, much like the golf and tennis clubs of today. The recreational canoe market suffered through the Depression of the '30s and never quite recovered from it. During World War II, materials and metals were absorbed by the war effort and the quality of canoes suffered. For a time steel canoe tacks and bolts had to be used because of the shortage of brass. The post-war economy did little to improve the canoe-building business.

Even during the war, anticipating a need for new markets after the war, Grumman Aircraft Company began working with the Alcoa Company to develop a practical aluminum canoe. In 1945 they produced a thousand canoes, 13' long, each weighing 38 pounds, priced slightly more than a wooden one. Soon the canoe manufacturing was separated from the aircraft operation, production rose, quality increased, and the price fell below that of a wooden canoe. It wasn't long before Grumman was the canoe king — until plastics took over the market in the '70s.

By the mid-1950s most of wooden canoe shops had closed or moved on to other products. Penn Yan of New York, Thompson Brothers and Shell Lake of Wisconsin, Skowhegan and Kennebec of Maine, and Robertson and Arnold of Massachusetts were out of business or not building canoes anymore. The only large, well-known companies to survive were Old Town, Chestnut, and the White Canoe Company, although White was to remain a marginal concern until the late '70s.

In the '50s White and Old Town greatly expanded their building of lapstrake and strip-built runabouts, and began experiments with fiberglass. White Canoe was the first to list a production fiberglass canoe in its catalog in the early '60s. But through a series of ownerships, the White Company had a steady decline until their major manufacturing product was reflective road signs. Boat construction was limited to a small number of fiberglass models build in the off season.

Clint Tuttle was able to obtain four of the original wooden canoe forms (20', 18-½', 16', 14') from the White Canoe Company in 1972. Clint started the Island Falls Canoe Company in Island Falls, Maine, building the wood-canvas canoes that had made the White Canoe Company famous. In 1974 Clint moved to Lubec, Maine, to be an instructor in a vocational boatbuilding program. In 1975, the authors, who were students of Clint, purchased the canoe company from Clint and in 1977 moved the business to Atkinson, Maine, a small town east of Dover-Foxcroft.

The E.M. White wood-canvas canoes have survived to be the last of the early canoe designs still being built today.

Through the '50s and '60s, Old Town Canoe struggled to carry on its tradition of wooden boats and canoes; even as late as 1971, wooden canoes, square-enders, war canoes, and wooden dinghies took up a major portion of its sales catalog. The popularity of the low-cost fiberglass models could not be suppressed, however, and in the 1972 catalog only six wooden canoe models were offered — two pages out of the 24-page catalog. But Old Town Canoe continues to maintain a small part of its excellent woodworking shop to produce a limited number of wooden canoes.

Over the last 30 years the reputation of the wood-canvas canoe has suffered at the hands of ignorant sporting writers and publications with little or no experience with or knowledge of wooden boats. But there has been a growing number of people recently who have rediscovered not only the romance of the wood-canvas canoe, but also the desirable qualities that are not found in canoes built with other materials. They find that the wood canoe is much more durable than the proponents of the synthetic materials lead people to believe. Accompanying this revival has been a resurgence of wood and canvas builders, but in most cases the secrets, skills, and knowledge of the old-timers were not able to be passed along to the new builders. Almost every new builder has had to go through a difficult and painful period of self-education trying to rediscover that knowledge. But a growing number of them have survived long enough so that today, there is a variety of quality wood-canvas builders who keep the craft and the canoe alive.

Canoe Materials 3

Arborvitae, the tree of life, more commonly known as northern white cedar, displays all the properties which make it ideal for the construction of canoes. It is no accident that this northern conifer was used throughout its natural range in the framing and planking of the native Indian bark canoes. It is likewise no coincidence that the wood-canvas canoe industry was born and nurtured in a region where lumber from this cedar was plentiful. Today it is still unsurpassed wherever it is available in long, clear lengths for planking, and even in relatively short stock for the milling of ribs. However, the availability of select lumber of this variety seems to shrink each year, and it is all but impossible to find outside its natural range. Accesss to suitable white cedar is still possible for builders living in a belt from the Maritimes through Ontario in Canada, and in the United States from northern New England, through upstate New York, Michigan, and as far west as Minnesota.

Cedar

Cedar is not an especially strong softwood, when compared to the spruces or hemlock for example, but the fibers are both tough and flexible, and the wood bends easily when either boiled or steamed. It is extremely lightweight as well, and displays less shrinkage and swelling than any other softwood once it is initially dried. Additionally, arborvitae is resistant to decay; so resistant in fact, it is commonly the choice for fence posts and outdoor furniture. As though these weren't qualities enough to recommend it for canoe building, the wood has rich tones and blonde color variations that make it especially attractive.

Finding clear planks of the white cedar lumber over 10-12' in length is rare even in the best cedar country — unless you are willing to select and cut the trees yourself; but although full-lenth planking would be ideal in a canoe, it is not an absolute requirement. If you can obtain good, clear white cedar in 6', 8', and 10' lengths, you will have very suitable material for planking the hull. If you can afford to be fussy, insist on rift- or quarter-sawn grain for your planking. Not only is it stonger, but it is more stable, making it less prone to swell and shrink and eventually warp, a problem sometimes encountered with flat-grain stock. The grain pattern of the ribs is not quite so critical. Traditionally boat ribs are bent on the flat grain, because they bend more easily in this configuration, and are less apt to split when pierced by the relatively large fastenings. With the wide, flat canoe ribs, neither of these points has much merit, so if you have a choice, quarter-saw your rib stock as well and it will result in a little extra strength in the hull.

If white cedar simply isn't available to you, you needn't give up the idea of building a canoe. There are several good substitutes that can produce very satisfactory results. Because of availability problems, the large manufacturers of canoes began importing western red cedar to use as planking as early as the 1910s. The long lengths they were able to

Flat or rift sawn lumber (left) and quarter sawn board (right) as they come from the log. The vertical grain of the quarter sawn stock shrinks less in width, and more evenly to prevent warping.

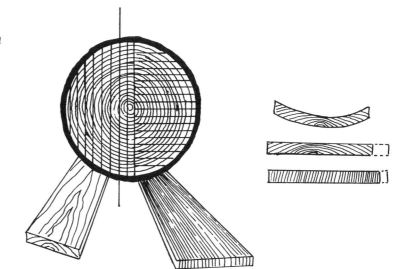

Variations in grain in white cedar planks.

obtain made planking the hulls a quick and simple matter, and the rich color of the wood made very attractive canoes. Furthermore, the red cedar was available quarter sawn, resulting in very stable planking that seldom cupped or warped even after years of use. The only real disadvantage a builder encounters with red cedar is its comparative brittleness, and even this deficiency is scarcely noticeable except in canoes that see a lot of action in rapids and shallow quickwater. Red cedar has also been successfully used as rib stock, but it is much more difficult to bend than white cedar, with a far greater incidence of failure under similar conditions.

Atlantic white cedar, often called Virginia cedar or juniper, is widely available in long, clear lengths — usually flat-grain — has good resistance to rot, and is a stable and relatively lightweight wood. It has been employed successfully for both planking and ribs; but once again, it is definately a more brittle wood than *aborvitae,* to which it is not related.

The Other Canoe-Building Woods

Alaskan as well as Port Orford cedar are two other rot-resistant, straight-grained woods suitable for canoe building that are readily available to West Coast builders. Top-grade eastern (northern white or red) and Sitka spruce can yield long, ideally grained planks that are both heavier and stronger than those made from cedar. The low resistance to dry rot of these species, however, could result in a shorter lifespan for the canoe. But the Indians north of the cedar zone have for centuries ribbed and planked their canoes successfully with spruce.

Both eastern and western spruce make ideal gunwale stock, however, because their ratios of strength to weight are unsurpassed and they are available in long lengths. Spruce is also noted for its ability to take a fair curve and keep it (hence its popularity as battens for lofting), a characteristic that makes it superior even to tougher woods such as white ash for inwales. Ideally, inwales are milled so the long vertical grain appears along the top and bottom of the rail, with the flat grain on the sides. Because of its lightness, spruce can also make an effective outwale, but it certainly is not as wear resistant as some of the hardwoods, so here we have a good application for white ash. Honduran mahogany is a dense, wear-resistant wood, traditionally used for outwales because of its hardness and rich contrasting color; black cherry may be similarly employed to good advantage. Because lightness is such an important characteristic in a canoe, perhaps it is better to save your oak for some more appropriate application, although otherwise it will make suitable outwales. Whenever possible, both in- and outwales should be milled from full-length stock; the inwales almost certainly, because they are primary structural members that hold the whole framework together. Fortunately, the above-mentioned species are still widely available in the required lengths from mills and specialty lumber dealers.

White ash is an excellent wood for making stems, because it is a fairly easy wood to bend and doesn't discolor in the process. It is tough and flexible, but unfortunately not especially resistant to decay. It is also the traditional choice for thwarts, yokes, and decks, but black cherry also holds up well, and its rich color contrasts nicely with the blonde shades of the canoe's interior. The seat frames should be made from a matching or complementary wood.

Selecting the stock for these parts with an eye towards color and grain pattern can go a long way toward achieving a balanced, attractive appearance to the finished boat. Should the builder have a flare for distinctive details in exotic woods, his efforts can be richly rewarded if he applies his talent to the making of these less critical canoe parts.

Clear cedar planking this long is worth protecting with a good guard dog.

The canoe's appearance can be enhanced by choosing a striking piece of stock for the decks, such as this dark, curly ash. Mahogany outwales define the canoe's shapeliness.

Fastenings

There are a number of different fastenings that come into play in the construction of a canoe, and to insure long service from your efforts as the builder, you will want to be sure they are all quality non-ferrous products — copper, bronze, or brass. The thin planking is clinch-fastened to the ribs by cut tacks. The best canoe tacks are cut relatively long and thin with a very sharp point to facilitate the clinching. Such tacks are available in brass in a number of lengths appropriate for different thicknesses of stock, and last indefinitely under normal use. Copper would be a better material for a canoe used exclusively or largely upon the salt water; lacking the zinc found in brass, it is far more resistant to electrolysis. Generally, however, it is difficult to obtain the proper tack in copper; the ones I have seen are too thickly cut and tend to split the frame when they are clinched over. You can still get good service from the brass tacks, even in salt water, if the canoe is kept well protected by varnish, and if you are careful never to leave salt water standing in the craft's interior.

A canoe tack with a slightly oval head is superior in this clinching process to the flat-headed variety. Use $3/4''$ or $11/16''$ tacks for canoes with standard construction, and $5/8''$ or $1/2''$ tacks when building a lightweight model. A tack that is too long for the job will be noticeably untidy in the interior, and quite possibly result in a splitting problem.

The ribs are held to the inside gunwales with nails. Far and away the best type for this job are the bronze boat nails with rings or ridges along the shank. These have superior holding power to any other variety for their size, resulting in few split rib tops during the framing process. A $7/8''$ 14-gauge nail is ideal for use in a standard canoe. The same type of nail is the best choice for nailing the ends of the planking to the stems. Here again, however, it may be difficult to find them in the proper size. Sometimes $5/8''$ or $1/2''$ 16-gauge nails can be purchased and put to this use, but even these are large when you consider the number of fastenings that will be driven into the stem. Most of the factories used 18-gauge steel wire nails for this purpose, and although the heads soon deteriorated, I have never seen a case where the planking had even begun to let go as a result.

Bronze or brass flat-head wood screws are the standard fastening for attaching the outside gunwales. I normally use 1-$1/2''$ No. 8's, countersinking them until the head of the screw sits just barely beneath the surface of the wood. Naturally, a shorter screw is more appropriate on a lightly built canoe.

The thwarts and seats are bolted to the inwales, and since there are frequently as many as 20 of these fastenings

Various fastenings employed in canoe construction, including ring nails and tacks.

Three suitable bolts for attaching thwarts. Although by far the stronger, the ¼″ carriage bolt also requires a larger hole in the inwale. The machine screw has a slotted top and requires a finish washer.

in the rails of the canoe, it is critical to use the lightest bolt suitable for the job. A ³/₁₆″ (10-24) bronze carriage bolt is normally strong enough for this purpose and requires a considerably smaller hole than the ¼″ size. Flat- or oval-headed machine screws (which are actually bolts) of this same size are also suitable, but must be used with finish washers to seat properly. I personally find that the big washer and the slotted head detracts from the clean sweep of the gunwales, although this is not a serious problem. The distinctive diamond-headed bolts, a trademark of an Old Town canoe and still available today from that company, are made of brass and have ⁷/₃₂″ shanks. I have seen hundreds of Old Towns in all sorts of repair, and cannot remember a single incidence of bolt failure, which would indicate that they have plenty of strength for the job.

Of course there is nothing save tradition that says stainless steel fasteners wouldn't do the job even better than the ones mentioned above. Stainless is certainly stronger than either brass of bronze, the new alloys all but indestructable. But appearance-wise — at least to a confirmed traditionalist such as myself — the glaring silver look of stainless steel has no place on a wood-canvas canoe.

The other materials you will be needing for the canoe —canvas, filler, marine finishes, and seat materials — will be discussed later in the book in the appropriate sections. The recommendations set forth above are based upon both the highest tradition of the industry and my own experience as a professional builder and enthusiastic paddler. But it is not to say that lacking access to any of these materials, you will not be able to obtain sustitutes that could work very well for you.

B.N. Morris Canoe Company

Some of the highest-quality wood-canvas canoes were built by the B.N. Morris Canoe Company of Veazie, Maine, a small town three miles north of Bangor. The company had a 30-year career that ended prematurely over 60 years ago. The Morris name and the fine canoes slipped into obscurity until the recent wooden canoe revival affored the pioneer company recognition and admiration again.

As well known as the company once was, hard facts about B.N. Morris are now difficult to find. Morris was one of the very early wood-canvas canoe companies, but how early is difficult to determine. A review of the company's publications suggests that different founding dates were claimed at various times. In 1912, it was reported to have started sales in 1891. In 1908, the company boasted it had built canoes since 1887; and in 1917 it claimed to have been manufacturing since 1882. The most commonly accepted date is 1887, which would have been when Bert Morris, the founder, was 21 years old.

Whatever date he started, Bert N. Morris started building canvas canoes at his family home in Veazie by using the Indian birchbark method. Only a few canoes were built using this method, however, and he quickly switched to the new method of building over a form. The first factory for what was originally called the Veazie Boat Company was a small, four-story building. Materials were milled on the bottom floor and passed up to the next floor, where the canoes were built. Each stage of construction took the canoes a floor higher, until they were finished and passed back down all four floors to be shipped. A larger factory was soon built, which was expanded and added upon as business progressed, resulting in a hodgepodge of various-sized wood-frame structures. Employment rose from a handful in the 1890s to 35 in 1910 to almost 75 by the time a fire destroyed the factory in 1920.

Morris canoes were aimed toward the turn-of-the-century recreational canoeing market and not the guides and woodsmen who wanted a less glamourous craft. His canoe designs soon departed from the style of the local bark canoes and became wider, fuller, and more stable with graceful, high, sweeping ends. The shapeliness, style, and workmanship of the Morris canoes and boats made some of the most picturesque craft that were ever built with this construction style.

The most unique construction characteristics of the Morris canoes was a nontraditional softwood (cedar) stem tht was almost 3" wide at the bottom of the canoe. On this "splayed" stem was a rectangular brass tag with a four- or five-digit serial number. There are several theories as to dating the canoes from the serial number; none have proven completely correct. The number may be a code or it may have been stamped on in numerical order as the canoes were produced. Other unusual characteristics of Morris canoes were copper stembands actually riveted through the stem, keels that were fastened at every rib, and the inwales notched to receive the top of the ribs.

A fire destroyed the factory in 1920 — a suspected case of arson. A case was never proven against the suspect, who was later found guilty of a separate case of arson and spent many years in a mental institution. At the age of 54, Bert did not feel he could rebuild the uninsured factory, so he set up a small one-man shop beside his house, where he built a limited number of canoes until his death in 1940. Much of the factory's material that was saved was sold to Old Town Canoe. Bert also worked for Old Town for a number of years, both at Old Town and from his home shop. One style of canoe he built for Old Town was an all-wood racing canoe, with ¼" cedar planking, ⅜x⅝" elm ribs, and maple decks. In a letter to builder Joe Seliga of Ely, Minnesota, in 1938, Bert identified three canvas models of canoes he was building in this limited way.

One result of the unfortunate fire was that his foreman, Walter Grant, moved to Waterville and became the superintendent of the Kennebec Canoe Company. He later went on to start the Skowhegan Canoe Company of Norridgewock. Grant's sister had married E.M. White and his twin brother worked for White all his life. A family reunion of Grants at one time would certainly have held much of the canoe-building information of Maine.

Bert died at age 74; there was no immediate family to receive the remaining Morris forms and records, so almost all of them disappeared and have yet to be found.

Shapes & Lines

4

The shape of a canoe, or the way its "lines" come together, determines both how the canoe will handle under various conditions and what it will look like. Generally, it is the shape on and beneath the surface of the water (below the waterline) that influences the performance characteristics, and the lines above water that determine the styling and to some extent the capacity of a particular model. It helps to know a little about the shapes of canoes before you consider building one, and you don't have to hold a degree in naval architecture to understand the fundamentals.

There are three basic views or perspectives from which to evaluate the lines of any boat. If you were to stand well back from the center of a canoe sitting right side up on a pair of sawhorses, you would be looking at the canoe's profile. The profile view best indicates the configuration of the keel line, the curve of the stem, and the sweep of the gunwales or the sheerline. From the performance aspect, the keel line is of the greatest importance. Occasionally you'll see a wood-canvas canoe with a keel that is perfectly straight. If you were to compare it with a parallel and level baseline of some sort, you couldn't detect the slightest rise in it the entire length of the bottom until the stems actually began their curve. A canoe with a keel line that rises slightly toward the ends — an inch or two at the beginning of the stems — displays what canoeists call rocker. A keel line that rises rapidly from the center towards the ends to a height of several inches is heavily rockered. The "hogging" of the bottom is just the opposite configuration. A canoe is hogged if the keel line actually dips down toward the ends from a highpoint amidships; this is usually a sign of a poorly manufactured or tired old canoe, rather than an intentional design feature, because it does nothing positive for the canoe's performance.

A straight keel line is designed for flatwater paddling, and because it helps keep the canoe on a straight course

Profile View

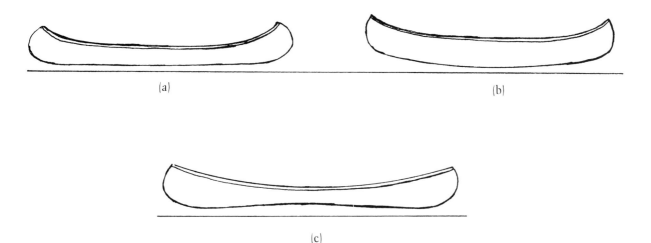

(a)

(b)

(c)

Profiles showing keel lines: (a)straight, (b)rockered, (c)hogged.

(tracking), it can be helpful to inexperienced paddlers who otherwise might have to exert considerable energy just keeping to their course. On the debit side of the ledger, this same characteristic severely limits a canoe's responsiveness when it comes time to turn it. When up to speed, it can act like a freight train on its tracks, and no light maneuver with the paddle is going to quickly bring it about. Such sluggishness can be disheartening to an accomplished paddler on flatwater, and in rapids, where quick maneuvering can be crucial, it is a trait which can be downright dangerous.

On the other hand, the severly rockered canoe in experienced hands can be spun like a top, almost in place, and with ease perform the maneuvers coveted by today's freestyle paddlers on flatwater while at the same time behaving well in the tight spots in a whitewater situation. Even a paddler of average ability, however, can have difficulty getting one of these banana boats to stay on a straight course between point A and point B.

The hull with moderate rocker tends to average out these extremes. With a little practice, almost anyone can get such a canoe to track reasonably well; yet it is also possible to execute graceful and decisive turns at the dock to impress those ashore. This same boat will allow the canoeist to make the occasionally necessary quick maneuver in quickwater, yet it can be held without great effort in a line parallel to the current for ferrying across the river to a safe channel on the opposite side.

The sheerline in profile can afford you further indications of a particular canoe's merits and limitations. The height of the sides, for example, helps to determine the safe load capacity of a hull, although it is by no means the only factor. This height of the sides, along with the surface area of the bow and stern is, however, the chief determining factor of the extent the canoe will be affected by cross-winds. A high-sided canoe with high ends is obviously going to be more difficult to manage in a stiff wind than is a low-sided craft with modest ends, especially if the canoe is lightly loaded. However, the deeper canoe will be the dryer one in really tough going whether you are caught out in a lake in a squall or running through haystacks in a rapid, and this is a feature that could someday save your life. Exactly where the sheerline attains its height above the waterline is also a factor. When a canoe is descending heavy water in a rapid, the water generally tries to climb aboard in the forward quarters of the boat, if it is going to, just about where the bow paddler is kneeling. Seldom will it come pouring in right over the bow, or amidships where most of the wave has been flattened out or turned back by the increasing width of the hull. The same is true when going to windward on a rough lake; the oncoming waves find the canoe most vulnerable in the foward quarters, just about at the bowman. This being the case, a moderate rise to the sheer, beginning at the center of the boat and gaining gradually all the way to the tip of the bow, can be more effective in repelling water than one that runs flat for most of its length then suddenly flares up into a high bow. At the critical point, near the bow seat, the more moderate sheer-line has already gained a couple inches in height above the waterline, while the other has basically the same freeboard in the quarters as it does amidships. For the most part, however, the sheer is the product of styling and very often reflects what a builder thinks looks attractive as much as it does practical considerations. The shape of the bow is also a matter of taste and tradition, not that there is anything wrong with that. If the Indians had built their boats strictly with an eye toward utility, and had never exercised their artistic talents, their lovely designs would have been as dreary as some of today's canoes, designed by obsessive performance engineers or computer models without any regard whatever for appearance. Basically, there has been very little new in bow shapes for hundreds of years. If you consider the stem profiles of the various Indian canoes developed across the continent, you will see that they run the whole gamut from essentially no bow at all to the immense, fully curved bows of the later Ojibway canoes, with everything in between — be it flared, plumb, or curved back.

Thompson Brothers Boat Manufacturing Company

The Thompson Brothers Company is unique among the early manufacturers of wood-canvas canoes. The company was established by an experienced professional boatbuilder who also happened to have good business skills. Although canoes played a major role in getting the company established, emphasis gradually shifted to speed- and powerboats. While many canoe companies used powerboats as a sideline, not many were able to become as successful as Thompson Brothers with these larger craft.

In 1904 Peter and Chris Thompson started building all-wood canoes in the family barn near Peshtigo, Wisconsin. For over 14 years, Peter had been employed by various quality wooden boat- and canoe-builders before returning home to start this business. The Thompson family must have been very close because within three years, four other brothers had joined the company along with several uncles and cousins.

The brothers rapidly expanded into wood-canvas canoes and all-wood rowing craft, skiff, barges, and inboard launches. By 1910 a large factory was built in town, producing a wide variety of boats. To maintain quality, the brothers felt each man should specialize in one style of boat or canoe and build only that craft. They also felt that factory-direct sales would keep the price of their boats lower by eliminating the middle man. As production increased, however, retail outlets became necessary to expand their market.

The canoes built early in the Thompson Company's history were noted for being of better quality than those built during the later period after the 1940s. The three most popular canoe models were the all-wood "anti-leak" model and the wood-canvas "Indian" and "Hiawatha" models. The construction of the canvas canoes incorporated many wooden boatbuilding techniques not common to most other wood-canvas canoes. The Indian model was noted for beveled-edged, overlapping planking. The E.M. White Company of

Maine was the only other company that lapped its planking. The lap prevented grit and sand from working between the seams and lodging between the canvas and the wood hull. The Hiawatha planking was narrow with beveled edges; this was supposed to make a smoother hull.

With the increase in the recreational boating field in the 1920s, a second large factory was opened in Cortland, New York. This plant produced inboard and outboard speedboats. It was also operated by one of the Thompson brothers and was active until 1956.

Canoe production declined in the 1930s, but in the late '30s the U.S. Forest Service ordered many rugged "camp" canoes, extending the company's canoe-building activity. By 1946, Thompson was advertised as "the world's largest manufacturer of outboard motorboats" and only one canoe model, the "Ranger," was being offered. In 1954, four of the Thompson brothers were still with the company — which had produced over 250,000 boats and canoes.

Unfortunately, it was not until the 1930s that the company began to use serial numbers and nameplates to identify their craft. The last year a wooden canoe was listed in the company's catalog was 1956, but it was still available until 1959. For a few years in the early '60s Thompson produced a fiberglass canoe, but even that was eliminated in the mid-'60s and the history of canoe building by the Thompson Brothers came to an end. Production of other boats continued to increase with a peak employment of 182 workers when the last Thompson brother sold the company to Saul Pudek in 1966. Pudek turned the comany toward large-scale fiberglass production, and even the other wooden boats were eliminated. In 1977, the company was sold to a St. Louis firm that moved the company to its current location in St. Charles, Michigan, where larger inboard-outboard runabouts and cruisers are manufactured.

Plan View

If you were to look down into a canoe from a vantage point such as a bridge, you would be enjoying what is known as the plan view of the craft. From above it is easy to see just what the canoe's beam is, how fine or full the ends are, and how the two extremes come together. Fast canoes are generally narrow for their length and display a fine entry — the end of the bow where it meets the water is the point of a sharp V that very gradually widens as it approaches the quarters. Such an entry disturbs the water minimally, slicing the medium and parting it, rather than plowing through.

A large-capacity freight canoe, on the other hand, will be considerably wider amidships, and it will carry these proportions the full length of the canoe to a full bow. This volume results in buoyancy that gives the canoe the large carrying capacity necessary for its work. The full bow also rides safely up on heavy water, where a fine-bowed boat might cut through, fill, and swamp. Most traveling canoes, whether Indian, cruising, or guiding in origin, are actually blends averaging out the two extremes. Wilderness travelers encounter all types of conditions, have varying capacity requirements at different times, yet must cover long distances. Thus they required a combination of the traits of these two very different types of canoes. The canoes of the Indians evolved naturally over hundreds of years to fulfill these requirements, but the manufactured canoes of the guides were designed with their specific needs in mind.

In general what these hybrid canoes had in commom was a moderately wide bottom amidships (it became very wide later on in some of the guide canoes), which had good initial stability and would carry a good load when necessary without drawing much water. Yet since long distances were often traveled and speed was important, the entries were kept narrow. In the plan view the bows of these canoes often displayed a hollow or reverse curve entry, which was necessary in order to flare the canoe out to its substantial width in the quarters.

Some designs are not symmetrical in plan view in order to fill certain requirements. When the outboard motor became popular on the larger rivers in the East, for example, freight canoes were designed that had conventional bows, but whose stern sections were purposely blunt and bulbous. This extra buoyancy aft was necessary to accommodate the outboard motor and the operator who was confined to the stern in order to run the thing. Many high-tech racing designs and free-style canoes of today take advantage of assymmetry to achieve specific performance qualities.

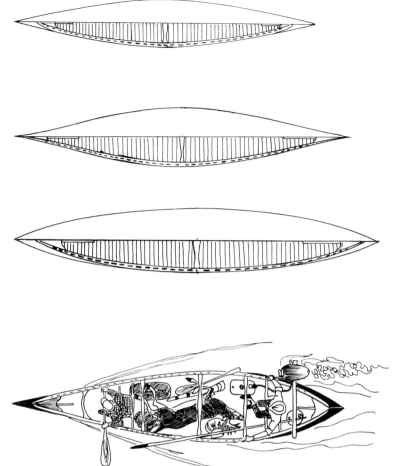

Plan views of three canoe types: top, Canadian shield cruising canoe; middle, Maine guide canoe; bottom, freight canoe.

An assymetrical freight canoe, designed to accomodate the weight of the outboard motor and operator well aft.

Cross-Sectional View

The view of a canoe that reveals the most information in respect to its performance is the end-on cross-sectional view. When these cross sections or stations are superimposed one over the other, you have what a marine achitect or loftsman would term the body plan. Naturally, you do not see these cross sections when you view the canoe from the end. The most you can perceive clearly is the shape of the canoe at its widest point, and the stem, with the foreshortened gunwale line connecting the two. But if you were to take your chainsaw and cut the canoe up into 16" sections — these sections viewed separately, then stacked together would afford you a lucid view of the changing shapes that make up a hull. The basic characteristics would jump out at you. Right away you would see whether the boat was flat, shallow-arched, or round-bottomed at each particular station. You would also see whether the sides were straight (vertical), flared out, or curved in at the sheer in the configuration known as tumblehome.

Cross sectional views showing different bottom configurations: (a)flat, (b)shallow arched, (c)modified "V", (d)round.

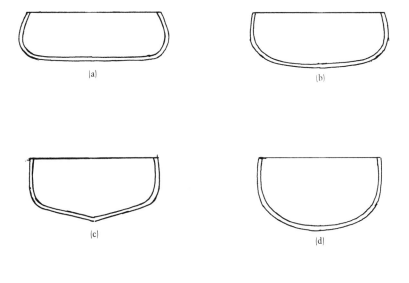

Most canoes have advantages as well as disadvantages. The round bottomed canoe(top) with the same load will draw more water than the beamier flatter bottomed canoe, but in a sea(bottom) it may be the drier canoe.

The shape of the bottom is perhaps the best single indicator of the canoe's handling characteristics. A wide, flat, or nearly flat bottom amidships indicates a shallow-draft canoe with good stability and a large carrying capacity. Such designs were favored by guides in Maine and on the salmon rivers of New Brunswick. Shallow water in the summer months required a canoe that would not draw more than a few inches of water even with a pretty good load aboard. During the hunting season a Maine guide might expect to carry his client, gear, and food for up to a couple weeks' comfortable living in the woods, with the possible additions of a large buck and a black bear at the end of a trip. A wide, flat-bottomed canoe of 20' would carry all this without requiring a foot of water to do it in. Such canoes were seldom very deep, usually just 12", because

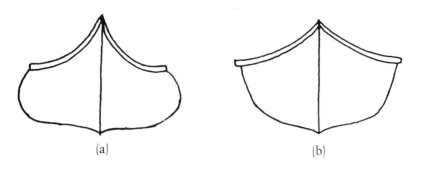

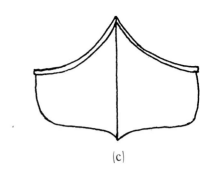

End views showing side configurations: (a)tumblehome, (b)flare, (c)straight.

their buoyancy allowed them to maintain plenty of freeboard even when loaded. The flat bottom had the additional advantage of providing excellent stability. This was also critical when you consider the guide was often standing in the stern of the canoe wielding his setting pole, while a passenger in the bow, probably totally inexperienced, was moving around trying to fish.

A bottom with a shallow arch in it makes a superior paddling canoe, and a round bottom results in even greater speed. This ease of paddling comes at the expense of initial stability, however, and a canoe with a pronounced round bottom can be very tender, even tippy when lightly loaded. Such a design often displays good "secondary stability," however, which means that once the canoe rolls well up onto its side, it once again achieves a stable position, which can be maintained by an experienced paddler indefinitely. A novice, unfortunately, unaccustomed to checking his own momentum as he goes over, can very easily overcome this secondary stability and find himself in the water alongside his inverted canoe.

The cruising canoes favored in the Canadian Shield country were similar to the Native American canoes of the region and generally were of moderate width, shallow-arched or round-bottomed, and deep — making them fast, maneuverable, and dry. The large lakes and deeper rivers of the Shield wilderness made draft a minor consideration.

The distinctive tumblehome of the sides of many traditional canoes can be very attractive, and because the sides are arched, such a configuration is structurally stronger than either a straight- or flare-sided arrangement. Tumblehome likewise makes paddling — especially for a kneeling bowperson of modest stature — somewhat easier because the gunwales are tucked in a little closer. The disadvantage of tumblehome is that in choppy conditions waves tend to follow the curve around to the sheer and toss what water they can spare into the canoe. A flare-sided canoe, almost always associated with a round bottom, is most effective at "knocking down" the chop before it can enter the canoe. Additionally, a flare-sided design actually gets more stable the more heavily it is loaded because the wetted surface increases the deeper the canoe sits in the water. Finally, the flared configuration displays the best secondary stability characteristics.

This has been a very brief introduction to some of the basic design features that determine a canoe's performance, so that you might at least recognize them when you encounter them on various canoes. Obviously other factors, notably length and weight, play important roles along with shape in determining how a canoe will ultimately perform, and help define a particular design's limitations. A good lines plan will clearly show all three views of the canoe and allow you to see at a glance if the model is likely to display the characteristics that would make it a suitable canoe for you. The best way to understand exactly how these features affect a canoe is to paddle as many different designs as you possibly can. Your perception of just how various characteristics interact may be pure speculation until your understanding is reinforced with actual experience. Since the combinations are so numerous, you would do well to supplement this hands-on experience with a look at some of the more successful traditional canoes, especially the ones that were favored for the type of canoeing you are interested in. Usually a canoe model was successful and sought after, year after year, for good reasons. Familiarity with the best of them, coupled with a basic understanding of why they perform as they do, should give you as the potential builder, the proper background for selecting an existing design, or even designing your own canoe to best suit your needs.

Building Forms 5

The development of the solid, steel-banded form that made the production of the wood-canvas canoe feasible for the manufactuerers, makes the task that much more difficult for the amateur wishing to build a single canoe or two. If he plans to use a form to facilitate the job, he must invest at least as much time and money into the form itself as he later will in the canoe. It can be a major hurdle for anyone with either a restricting budget or limited spare time. One solution is to forget the solid form concept and set up a skeletal jig using the molds, a backbone, and ribbands running the length of the structure. Such jigs have been used for decades for all-wood canoes and small boats of all types. The ribs are bent either on the inside or the outside of the ribbands and the planking fastened to them as the ribbands are removed. This method requires that the clinch nails be backed up by an iron each time, and clamps are necessary to hold the planking in place while it is being fastened. It is no more difficult, however, than building most other small craft, and the results should be equivalent — but it is certainly more time consuming and awkward than building over the form.

Another approach is to get together with other canoeists in the region or talk the members of a local sportsmen's or environmental organization into mounting a joint effort: once the form has been produced, with the subscribing members sharing the work and expense, they can help one another building their canoes. In our area, several school districts have had forms built in industrial arts classes and these are used each year in adult education courses that run through the winter one or two evenings a week. It is a welcome resource for those beset by a long dark winter, and the resulting canoes are usually raffled off to interested students willing to pay the cost of the materials.

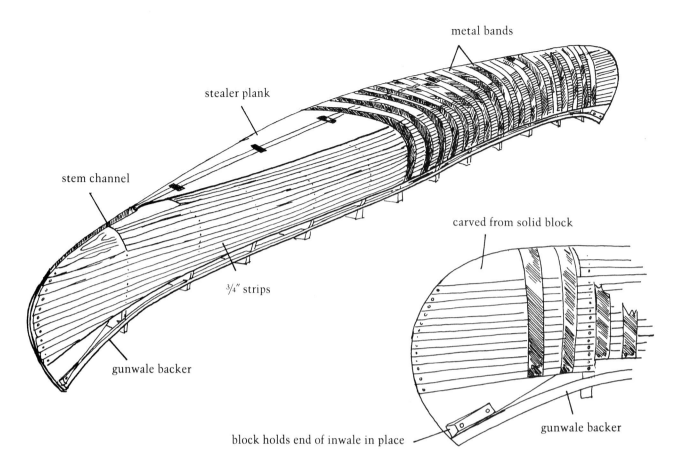

metal bands

stealer plank

stem channel

carved from solid block

³/₄" strips

gunwale backer

block holds end of inwale in place

gunwale backer

*A nearly completed form showing most
parts.*

Canoe Plans

However you plan to proceed, you will need a set of appropriate plans to make the station molds which, when set up along a backbone, give the canoe form its three-dimensional shape. A proper set of plans will show the canoe drawn out in all three views — plan view (bird's-eye), profile, and the cross-sectional half-breadths or "body plan" which is the view actually used in producing the molds. A table of offsets — the actual measurements of the various waterlines and buttocks — from established reference lines should also be included to cross-check information. If the plans you hope to use have all this information, you can be sure the designer or draftsman has gone through all the steps to insure accuracy. Beware of cheap plans that simply show the molds superimposed one over the other on a reduced grid that must be expanded to get the full-sized drawing. Not only is it next to impossible to do an accurate job enlarging the cross sections by this method, but it is a good indication that the perpetrator of the design either knew nothing about the established methods of taking and reproducing lines or was too lazy to bother. In all probability, the lines resulted from tracing the shapes from an existing canoe with no subsequent drafting steps to betray any mistakes or refine the dimensions. Plans sold by institutions such as the Smithsonian, the Adirondack Museum, and Mystic Seaport on the other hand, have been drawn by professionals, display all the views, have a corrected set of offsets, and can be depended upon to accurately reflect the craft they represent. The only drawbacks are that not all of these plans come with the individual stations drawn out full-sized on separate sheets, and the selection of available wood-canvas canoe designs is limited.

Lofting

If you already know something of drafting, lofting is simply performing the same exercises on a much larger scale — drawing the plan out full scale as opposed to say $\frac{1}{2}''$ = 1'. All that is required to accomplish this is a couple sheets of plywood painted white, some spruce battens, and an accurate set of offsets.

The study plans in this book, drawn by Rollin, have been fully drafted in all views and the offsets corrected from the final drawing. You can work from these with confidence or write him about a full-sized set for any of the three designs which include full-sized mold drawings on separate sheets. As a bonus, the molds have been reduced to accommodate the solid sheathing of the form as well as the dimensions of the canoe planking and ribs, and are ready to be laid out on the mold stock for cutting.

Molds

The molds themselves are cut from top-quality $\frac{3}{4}''$ plywood (birch is recommended) or pieced together in sections using dry $1\text{-}\frac{1}{2}''$ spruce lumber held firmly together with $\frac{1}{4}''$ plywood gussets at all the joints. The solid plywood molds are easier to make and for all practical purposes serve as well as those constructed of lumber. The spacing between molds should not exceed 18", 16" being about the ideal. Longer spans can result in a springy surface that oilcans when the tacks are driven home.

The molds are cut out on the bandsaw, faired exactly to the line, and set up along a 2x6 backbone for which they are notched, or fastened stripper-fashion onto a long flat base — normally a straight 2x8 lying flat. In either case, a string run end to end along the centerline ensures the molds are lined up properly, and a level is used to keep the molds plumb. Rollin's mold patterns are designed with a flat top

Molds notched to be set up on along backbone.

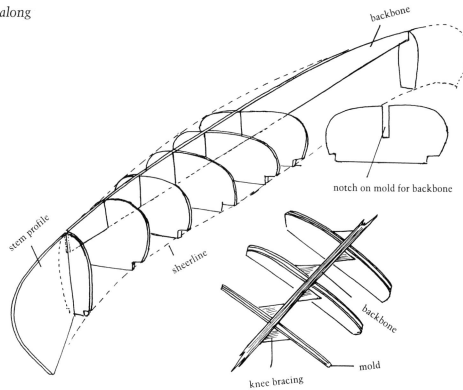

backbone

notch on mold for backbone

stem profile

sheerline

backbone

mold

knee bracing

representing a common waterline, making setup along the 2x8 relatively simple.

Because the molds diminish in size as they approach the ends, the strips that later make the form a solid structure will touch only the leading corner of the mold edge, unless each mold is beveled along this edge. Obviously, the bevelling will result in a firmer union of the strips and molds, although the alternate method is tolerable especially if the molds are made of solid spruce.

Once again, a good set of plans is essential if you elect to bevel the mold edges. The angle of the bevel for each station can easily be lifted from the profile view — otherwise it is guesswork.

Whether or not you bevel the molds will also determine their positions along the strongback. Beveled molds are set up ahead (closer to each end) of the actual station line, while molds without the bevel are set behind the station line.

Once properly set, each mold is firmly secured with the addition of little triangular knees to either the backbone (which slices through the notched molds in a vertical plane), or to the horizontally oriented 2x8. The shape of the ends of the canoe to be built will be determined by the

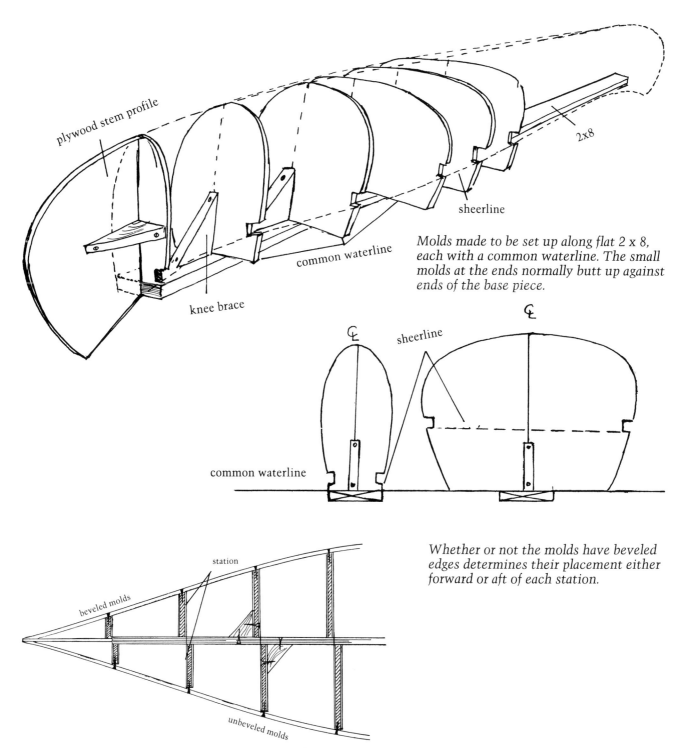

Molds made to be set up along flat 2 x 8, each with a common waterline. The small molds at the ends normally butt up against ends of the base piece.

Whether or not the molds have beveled edges determines their placement either forward or aft of each station.

stems, which are bent separately over another jig. Therefore it is not a requirement to reproduce the bow and stern of the canoe in full profile, as long as there is a provision for firmly positioning the stem itself. It is good practice, however, to cut the stem profile out of plywood and attach it to the first mold at each end by means of more of the little knee braces.

This form has both a vertically oriented backbone, and a flat 2x8 for holding the molds in place. Note knees for bracing.

Temporary ribbands are useful for keeping the molds square and plumb during setup.

Installing the stealer planks on either side of the backbone.

The first strips in place. The void between the first and second molds will be filled in by solid blocks of wood.

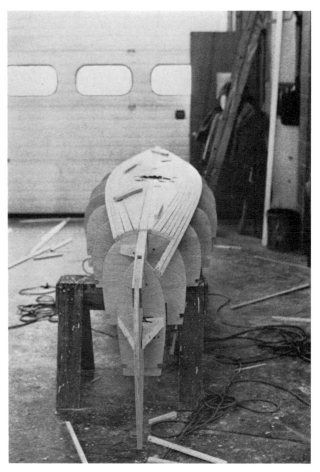

Before the strips are installed, the molds must be checked one to another to insure overall fairness. Spruce ribbands 1″ by ⅜″ are run from mold to mold the length of the canoe to facilitate this, as well as to firm things up temporarily. One or two ribbands along the bottom, another at the turn of the bilge, and one roughly paralleling the sheerline on each side should be plenty to verify the fairness of the structure. If everything is in order, the ribbands will lie sweetly along the row of molds without any distortions and without missing any of the mold edges. A hump in a ribband or space between the ribband and a mold usually indicates a problem, which should be corrected by some prudent shaving or the use of a shim. Don't ignore such information, because any neglected unfairness will be later reflected in the permanent strips.

Ribbands

You can use ¾″-square quality pine or spruce strips to sheathe the form, although heavier dimensions may be elected. They are attached to the molds with screws (the versatile 1-¾″ phillips-head sheetrock screws are ideal), but predrilling will be required wherever the strips are stressed by twisting. To make the strips come out as parallel as possible to the sheerline, and to save work, a pair of "stealer" planks may be fashioned and fit on either side of the centerline. The shape of these stealers is derived from differences in the form's girth amidships and at the start of the stems — 10″ or 11″ on the typical canoe. Each stealer is laid out on a ¾x6″ board the required length, using a batten to derive a fair curve, which will result in a plank 6″ wide amidships and ½″ wide at the ends. The curve is cut out on the bandsaw and faired to the line. The edge of the stealer against the centerline will of course be left straight, therefore a separate stealer is made for each side of the form.

The first strip is laid alongside the stealer, secured to the molds, and fastened to the stealer with either ring nails or more sheetrock screws 1-½″ long: each succeeding strip will be similarly fastened to the strip above it. Considerable twisting will be required to make the initial six or eight strips on each side conform to the form's shape. A "wrench" cut out of plywood with a square hole in it the size of the strips can be helpful in accomplishing the twist. Still, especially on canoes with a fine entry, it is better to end the first eight strips on the final or the next to the last mold at each end. As the amount of twisting decreases, the strips may be extended to run up alongside the bow profile and beveled at the ends for a close fit. The voids left by the shortened strips are eventually filled in with wedge-shaped blocks

Sheathing

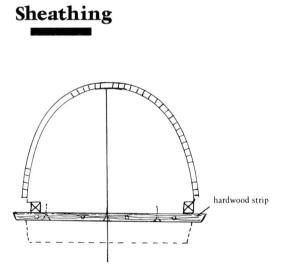

hardwood strip

Hardwood strips are added to the molds across the gunwale backers to make attachment of the gunwales easier.

that are fastened in place and carved to shape with a spokeshave to achieve the fine entry. The sides of the molds represent a curve so the strips will lie tightly against each other on the inside, while gaps will be evident along the outside surface. The gaps can be eliminated by carefully beveling the strips their entire length, but in fact this is a tedious, time-consuming process with no real advantage. The form must be build solidly, but it isn't necessary to make it watertight.

Because of the stealer planks the strips will reach the sheerline fairly consistently along the form's length, except on high-ended models, where the ends of the form are built up by increasingly shorter strips. The strips are brought to within an inch or so of the actual sheer, but further fiddling to match the sheerline exactly is largely a waste of time.

A channel to hold the flat run of the stem must be left at each end of the form along the centerline. The depth of the channel is determined by the thickness of the stem stock that will be used, minus the thickness of the proposed rib stock. The straight end of the stem should fit into the channel, with the notches for the ribs just showing above the surrounding wood. The notch gets shallower with more of the stem exposed as it approaches the very end until it disappears altogether at the end of the form, exposing the entire thickness of the stem which continues to curve around the stem profile on the outside surface.

The gunwales are recessed along the sheerline so the rib-side surfaces are flush with the surface of the strips. Notches must be cut on each of the molds to accommodate not only the gunwales but also the gunwale "backers," which are permanent 1"-square stringers running along the

Plywood "wrench" helps twist the square strips into place for fastening.

sheerline to which the inwales are secured. Here again a good set of plans will indicate the exact position, depth, and angle of the notches. Hooks may be fashioned and installed at each mold to hold the gunwales flush against the backers, or C-clamps may be used for this function, when it's time to build a canoe.

The form itself is faired and smoothed before the metal bands are installed. Use a spokeshave or block plane to knock down the inevitable ridges which are evident along the tighter turns of the shape. A good fairing tool is a 60-grit 6x48" belt from a stationary sanding machine, cut and extended to its full length with a pair of rough handles nailed at each end. Two persons, one on either side of the form, work this belt back and forth across the hull along the form's length, angling it to keep it flush against the form even in the quarters. When the form looks and feels fair, it should be carefully smoothed with a disc sander and finally a long-based orbital sander, or hand-sanded using a lightly padded block at least 8" long. A couple coats of varnish or at least some boiled linseed oil will afford some protection to the wooden structure.

Galvanized steel bands 2-³/₈" wide cut from 20-gauge stock are sufficient to turn the tacks for dozens of canoes. Heavier gauge is even more effective, but is difficult to form around the tight turns of some designs. The bands are spaced 4" on center, but this may be changed to better suit a particular model. Their position is marked along the centerline (the form is upside down in the building configuration), and the bands are predrilled to accommodate a screw

Metal Bands

Care is taken installing the gunwale backers.

The finished form, with strongback, stem, and gunwales in place. The metal bands are galvanized.

It is easy to see the function of the rail backer and stem slot on this older form. GC

on each stealer near the centerline. Hold the band in place and bend it around the hull. Its exact length may be determined at the lip of the final wooden strip near the sheerline. The band is taken to a bench where it is cut to length, allowing ½" extra on each end to be folded around the edge of the wood later, and two holes are countersunk and drilled for screws. Use 1" sheetrock screws and fasten them to the next to the last strip. The band is attached at the centerline, then bent around and fastened at the ends; the excess metal is folded around the edge of the wooden strip by striking it with a hammer.

As the compound curves develop in the quarters of the form, the ends of the bands will have a tendency to "cant" back amidships if the strips are to remain flush against the wood. The flat ribs will have this same tendency, so it is nothing to be concerned about. We will later discuss how tapering the ribs can do a lot to visually eliminate the effects of this rake. The bands are cut in two and attached separately on either side of the stem channel when the end section of the form is reached. In succeeding years, as the tacks take their toll on the galvanized surface, it will be necessary to keep the bands varnished in order to prevent rust from staining the ribs.

The Strongback

The ribs are held tightly down along the centerline of the canoe during the bending and curing process by a strongback — normally an 1-½x3" spruce member extending from stem to stem along the form's centerline. This is normally bolted down onto the form during these steps and braced from above during the planking process to eliminate holes in the planking that would have to be patched. Five tapped metal plates ⅜" thick are installed along the centerline between the metal bands to accept the bolts.

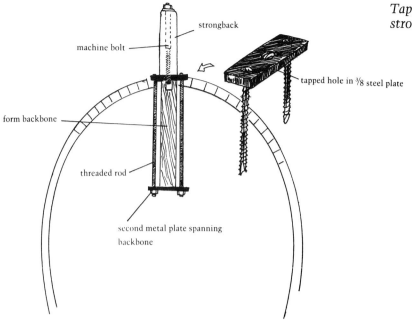

Tapped metal plate for bolting down strongback.

The tapped pieces are recessed into the wood and held securely in place by two lengths of threaded rod that extend down along the sides of the backbone inside the form, passing through complementary holes in a second metal piece that spans the bottom edge of the backbone. Nuts are threaded onto the protruding ends of the rods and snugged up against the lower metal plate (see diagram).

The convenience and long life of a well-built form surely justify all the work and attention that goes into its construction, and it will repay the builder each time a lovely and fair hull is removed from it. There is no more room for short cuts and sloppiness in its construction than in that of the subsequent canoes. Choose your lines carefully and lavish attention on the form — it will pay dividends in the form of handsome canoes for years to come.

6

Jerry's Construction Journal

April 15

It is the ides of April and above the poplar grove by the pond a pair of black ducks are banking for a landing on the patch of open water along the far shore. Optimists surely, because there is no breath of spring in the biting wind that's flattening last summer's unharvested timothy against the frozen earth. Only the willows, their supple branches already turning a light shade of green, are brash enough to proclaim that this is but a temporary setback, and winter is poised to concede and flee.

Bending Stems and Ribs

A quick fire of scrap in the barrel stove brings the shop to life, and by the time I've selected my rib stock and piled it on horses beside the table saw, I am able to remove my jacket and don the paint-and-filler-encrusted apron to begin work. It is now a week since I was last at work, bending the white ash stems for the 18'6" canoe. The 6'-long 1" stock was not seasoned when I ran it through the thickness planer to a thickness of 7/8". Because I like light-colored stems, I concentrate on the lighter wood along the edges of the flat-grained board, slicing off 7/8"-wide strips on the bench saw until I reach the chocolately brown heartwood. I get three strips from one side and four from the other, enough, given average success, to bend more than the four individual stems that will fit on the stem jig standing empty by the steam box.

The jig is made of good birch plywood, cut to the shape of the bows of my 18'6" E.M. White guide-model form. The bow is almost plumb, so the curves on the jig represents a slight exaggeration of the actual shape. This slight over-bend will allow for the tendency of the stem to straighten out a bit when it is removed from the jig after curing. Oddly enough, on stems with a fuller curve, this is seldom neces-

Bending a stem over the birch plywood jig. Note the thin batten used to prevent splitting. GC

sary. The greater arc seems content to retain the shape to which it has been coerced. Three bolts, passing across the face of the jig through holes in three pairs of tabs, hold the bent stems flush against the form. I use thin wooden battens to trap the wood against the shape as it is bent to prevent little imperfections in the grain from splitting off the outside surface of the stem as it is bent and developing into serious splits. One day I will replace them with permanent steel straps.

I use the same cedar steam box I will later employ for bending the ribs, and during the building season, I bend more stems each time I use the box to replace those I've removed and used. My steam box is made from ship-lapped cedar 8' long, the inside dimensions about 16" square. It is divided vertically into three levels by four sets of dowels that pass through the box from side to side. The ends, just inside the hinged doors, are further divided by vertical dowels of smaller diameter, forming little compartments wide enough to hold two ribs on end without crowding. By opposing the shorter ribs in one end of the box with the longer ones in the other end, I can easily get all the ribs for one canoe into the box at once. There is enough space over the topmost horizontal dowels to put stems or the ends of gunwales that need steam softening. An old-fashioned propane-fired plumber's torch heats the water in the steam chamber, which is merely an old stainless milking machine pail. The mouth of the pail fits snugly over a sort of flange around a hole in the bottom surface of the box. when running full bore, it fills the box with a good volume of wet steam, hot enough to require the use of work gloves when handling the stems. A steam-cleaning apparatus with a coil arrangement will provide the builder with greater volumes

Parts of a wood-canvas canoe.

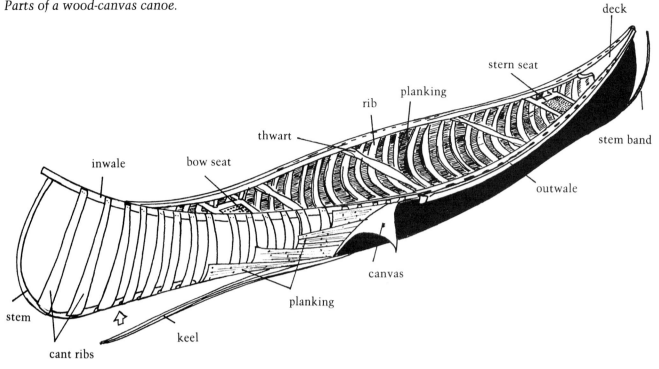

deck

stern seat

planking

rib

thwart

inwale

bow seat

stem band

outwale

canvas

stem

planking

keel

cant ribs

The plumber's propane torch and milking machine pail used to generate steam.

The cedar steam box is lowered onto the milking machine pail.

Partitions inside the steam box separate the ribs.

Chestnut Canoe Company

In Canada, the word canoe could almost be substituted for the name "Chestnut." The deep, maneuverable prospector and cruiser models have long been favored by seasoned canoeists in the vast Canadian Shield territory. For almost 50 years, Chestnut had a virtual monopoly on any large scale wood-canvas canoe building in the whole of Canada; but through a series of mismanagement steps, even the advantages were not enough to ensure the company's continued success.

Henry and William Chestnut set up a canvas canoe-building business around 1897 under the family hardware store name of R. Chestnut and Sons. They hired a local experienced boatbuilder to copy the Maine canvas canoes that were finding their way into the Chestnuts' hometown of Fredericton, New Brunswick. The company grew fast and the brothers sought experienced builders from Maine, resulting in at least one lawsuit with the Old Town Canoe Company (see page 33).

Chestnut's biggest competition in Canada came from the Peterborough Canoe Company, which had a long history of all-wood canoe building and tried to work into the new wood-canvas canoe market. In 1905 Chestnut obtained a Canadian patent on the wood-canvas canoe construction technique, and this prevented any other Canadian company from building canvas canoes. Peterborough took the case to court and lost. In its early catalogs Chestnut warned: "We hereby warn anyone in Canada against using our construction."

During the early years, the Chestnut brothers considered the canoe company little more than a hobby and did not want to deal with the business problems of retail sales, but the pressures grew because of the effectiveness of their patent. So in 1923, Chestnut turned to its stifled competitor, Peterborough, to form Canadian Watercraft Limited. Essentially the agreement allowed Peterborough to market the canoes built at the Chestnut factory. At one point these canoes were sold under all three names: Chestnut, Peterborough, and Canadian Watercraft Limited. To add to the confusion, Peterborough again began to produce their own wood-canvas canoes.

Two fires in the '20s almost destroyed the Chestnut company, but they made

of even hotter wet steam, and might be considered necessary for a large boat shop or manufacturer. So-called "superheated" steam has a very low moisture content, and is more suitable for baking than steaming wood.

A rule of thumb when bending wood is to allow one hour in the box (once full steam is generated) for each inch of thickness of the stock. This is a good place to begin, but in practice, I find my $7/8$"-square stems require a minimum of an hour and a half to soften properly. Because the stem stock is square, I am able to take best advantage of the ideal flat grain in each piece. Besides having the growth rings in the "flat" configuration, I further bend each piece toward "the center of the tree." This is a traditional practice, which although doesn't guarantee success, at least gives you something to fall back on when you can't decide which way you think will work best. Also, because my stock is square, I must take great pains when executing the bend not to twist the stem as I form it around the jig. I once bent stems double — a piece of wood the proper thickness, but slightly wider than two stems. Once bent and cured, these wide pieces were split on the bench saw into two identical stems. This flat configuration naturally resists twisting, but it was also much harder to bend and I would resort to boiling them to achieve a decent success rate. Boiling is an effective, alternative technique to steaming for gunwales and ribs as well.

It was a good day when I bent the stems for this canoe, and the first four pulled from the box bent like pasta around the form without a threat of breaking. One by one I bent them beneath their wooden battens, then locked them in place with wedges driven under the bolts. By today they are fully cured and ready to be used anytime.

If the canoe I was about to build had a sudden rise in the sheerline at the ends, I would also have pre-bent the gunwales. The jig for this task is similar to the one used for the stems, or it can simply be two pieces of plywood cut to the proper shape, connected by 1"-square hardwood crosspieces to which the gunwales may be clamped as they are bent. The slightly more elaborate version, complete with steel straps that trap the gunwales onto the surface of the jig, is a worthwhile investment if you are going to do this often.

White ash and cherry are the only popular gunwale woods that bend easily. Spruce and mahogany can both be troublesome, if you don't have a first-rate source of steam. For this reason many builders and restorers resort to boiling them instead. As with the stems, it is advisable to slightly overbend them to allow for the pieces relaxing when removed from the jig after a few days' curing. This can cause a bottleneck in your schedule if you haven't planned ahead, because the length of the gunwales makes it all but impossible to do both ends at once, especially if you work alone.

The rib stock I have selected is a full inch thick, rough, and a fraction over 5″ wide. Most of the boards are about 6′ long. By carefully choosing my cuts, I should be able to get four pieces of stock from each board. I'll need 60 ribs for the canoe, counting spares and cant ribs in the ends (I make 10 extra to be safe), and since I selected the stock myself at the yard, I am confident that the 16 pieces ready to mill (only 45 board feet of lumber) will suffice for my needs. The first cut slices the board in two lengthwise, yielding two 2-1/2″-wide strips. The next pass reduces this width to the final 2-1/4″ quicker and more accurately than would a jointer planer, but a thickness planer may be employed with the stock on edge to get the second smooth edge. I next hold the stock on edge and resaw each piece into two 7/16″-thick slices ready for planing on both sides. This canoe is to be built standard weight, and I will plane the stock to 5/16″ thickness. If it were to be built lightweight, the ribs could be as thin as 1/4″. A freight or expedition canoe, on the other hand, may require ribs 3/8″ thick. It is a strange thing (or more likely the result of manufacturing expedience) that canoe manufacturers, for the most part, used the same sized members in all their models whether 12′ or 20′ long. This made for consistency in production certainly, but is ridiculous when you consider the different structural requirements of the two extremes. A yacht builder, for example, would never use the same sized frames and planks on a 50′ sailboat as he would on a 22-footer. The results in the canoe industry were small canoes grossly overbuilt and much heavier than they needed to be for general use. (This may have had something to do with the public's eagerness to abandon the wood-canvas canoe in favor of the new aluminum versions when these became available.) E.M. White took exception to this practice and used smaller dimensions in the materials for some of his shorter models; he offered lightly built versions of his longer canoes to those who didn't need the same ruggedness in their boats as the guides. Chestnut of Canada responded to the opposite need — and provided cruising and guiding canoes build extra heavy for those who might require the extra beef.

There is a practical limit to just how light the parts can get and still allow the canoe to hold its shape, however. The bottom of the canoe, unless used only by a child, is going to have to support a paddler whose significant weight is concentrated in a small portion of the canoe. (This is a situation that does not have a parallel in the comparison with the yacht.) Therefore any length canoe framed with ribs

Harry Chestnut take his canoe business more seriously. Canoe designs were modified or improved, the forms were rebuilt, and the company recovered from the fires stronger than ever. The variety of canoes that Chestnut could produce seemed almost endless. There were over 60 forms, and in many cases two or three different styles of canoe could be built from each. A canoe could be built lighter, heavier, longer, deeper, shallower, square-sterned, V-sterned, finely finished, rough-keeled, or smooth-bottomed. Nearly each of these variations had an odd model name such as Henry, Parr, Kruger, or Boone; they were all 16′ "Ogilvy" models, each built a little bit differently.

The company enjoyed steady progress while the Chestnuts operated the factory. Harry Chestnut died in 1941 and ownership was passed on to several family members until 1954, when Peterborough finally bought the Chestnut Canoe Co. In 1958 Peterborough obtained a $350,000 loan using their Chestnut assets as collateral to build a new factory for strip-planked runabouts. By 1962 fiberglass had overtaken the runabout market, and Peterborough went out of business and defaulted on the loan. The bank ended up owning Chestnut, but by now the company was in a financially weakened condition and its marketing arms, Peterborough and the Canadian Watercraft Limited, had been lost. A series of government loans and several owners tried to keep the company operating, but the quality of the canoes dropped as new owners tried to produce volumes of canoes at prices competitive with synthetic models. Chestnut was forced to close its doors in 1979.

The Chestnut canoe forms were dispersed across North America, and various builders began producing the different models. Former employees Don Fraser and Carl Jones have their own shops, producing limited numbers of some of the more popular Chestnut models. The company name and many more forms were purchased by an Ontario Indian tribe and eventually sold to Chestnut canoe enthusiast and historian, Ken Solway. Ken has started a shop in Toronto where he is producing the canoes that made Chestnut world famous.

less than ¼" thick, and planked with sheathing thinner than ⅛" is going to be severely stressed in the region of the paddler's knees. This stress can result in distortion of the hull that can become a permanent feature of the canoe after a surprisingly small amount of use. A "floor" rack can help disperse this concentration over a larger area, but the additional weight of such an option will probably be as great as more suitable ribs and planks would have been in the first place.

After planing my ribs to ⁵⁄₁₆", I carry the stock over to the radial arm saw for trimming to the proper length. I must use 15 or 16 different rib lengths to insure the excess at any frame is no more than 2" on either side; otherwise the tapers I will be cutting into the widths of the ribs at the ends will not be consistent. I do allow an inch or so extra at each end to facilitate bending and attaching the ribs to the gunwales. I take the extra time to stand up all the material against the wall so I can select and cut judiciously. I cut my longest ribs first and work to eliminate any imperfections in the grain or small knots as I work down the list. This extra effort pays off handsomely in the quality of the finished stock. I must also mark the center of each rib at this time and label each according to length.

Traditionally the ends of the ribs are tappered in width. It eliminates bulk and weight where is isn't needed, since the bottom of the hull must be stronger than the topsides. Although you sometimes encounter ribs that are tapered on both edges, the majority of canoes have ribs tapered only on the trailing edge (that edge facing amidships). Used in this manner, the taper visually reduces the effects of the pronounced "cant" or lean of the ribs in the quarters of the canoe, which is the result of bending a flat rib around a compound curve and keeping both edges flat against the

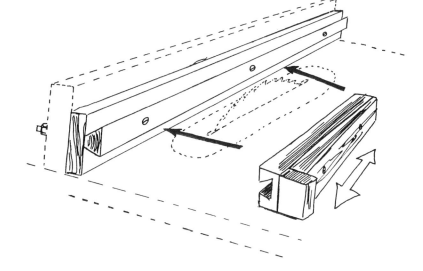

Sliding wedge device for tapering ribs.

The sliding wedge tapers the ribs consistently. GC

The ribs as well as the planking are pre-sanded on the drum sander. GC

Shaping the edges of the ribs on the inverted router.

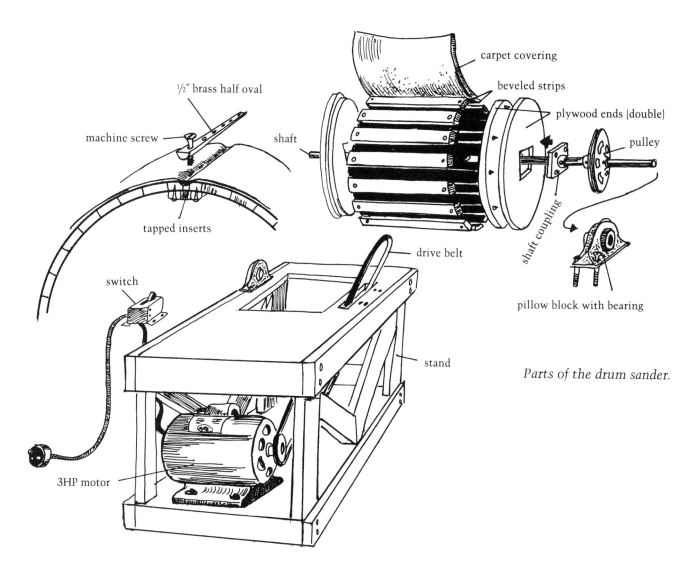

½" brass half oval

machine screw

shaft

carpet covering

beveled strips

plywood ends (double)

pulley

tapped inserts

shaft coupling

pillow block with bearing

drive belt

switch

stand

3HP motor

Parts of the drum sander.

form. The angle of the taper facing amidships makes the ribs appear plumb. If you prefer the rakish look of the canted ribs, either eliminate the taper, or face it toward the ends of the canoe. I taper the top 11" of my ribs to 1-5/8" using the bench saw and the sliding wedge device pictured in the diagram. The tapers appear rather angular on the flat ribs but miraculously disappear when they are bent onto the form. For a one-time project, it is just as easy to mark the tapers onto the ribs and cut them two at a time on the bandsaw.

White (as well as certain New Brunswick builders) tapered his ribs in thickness as well — saving weight in the process and insuring a very flat bottom on certain models. The old Whites had ribs that tapered in thickness from 5/16" or 3/8" in the bottom of the canoe to 3/16" at the gunwales. Personally I prefer the slight arch in the bottom, and that is what I get from the old flat-bottomed form when the ribs haven't been thinned at the ends. If the flat bottom is a characteristic you wish to replicate, the best method would be to construct a jig which raised the ends of the ribs slightly as they passed through the thickness planer. The meat should be removed from the backside of the rib.

I get plenty of use from the homemade drum sander in my shop (see diagram), using it to pre-sand the surfaces of all the ribs and planking and to help shape thwarts and paddles. I run the inside surfaces of each rib across it at this time using 120-grit XHD abrasive cloth to make them smooth without removing significant material. The ribs will suffer through the steaming and building processes and will later require sanding inside the canoe, but careful pre-sanding at this stage makes the job much easier. A light-grit belt on a stationary belt sanding machine serves just as well, and the pneumatic sanding drums now available can do a variety of jobs superbly when the amount of pressure in the drum is regulated.

The final step in the production of the ribs is shaping the edges. Square-sided or bevel-edged ribs detract from the finished appearance of the canoe in my view, yet a true radius loses some of the crispness I favor. To achieve the shape I prefer, I use the lower three-quarters of a cutter designed to make a ½" radius. This shapes the edges nicely without overdoing it. Lacking a proper shaper, I make do with an inverted router fastened to a bench surface, and a homemade fence. Shaping the straight edge of the ribs on such an arrangment is simple, but it takes a bit of practice to get the hang of smoothly shaping the tapered side. A little hand-sanding — necessary in any event — should smooth out any hard spots in the vicinity of the tapers.

After carefully touching up the edges of my ribs with sandpaper, I put them aside and concentrate on picking out the stock for planking. If I felt like working right up to the five o'clock whistle, I would have enough time to cut the stock to width, but it seems like a big project to launch late in the afternoon, and one that can easily be put off until tomorrow.

April 16

Clouds slipped in last evening as soon as the cold northwest wind died, and the temperature rose throughout the night. A warm, light rain is now falling and a ragged shroud of fog and mist is being swept gently across the fields, raked to shreds by the maples along the fencerows. Together they will take their toll on the few isolated windrows of snow that sprawl amoeba-like wherever a stone wall or a line of spruces has shielded them from the advancing sun. Spattered and befouled by mud and windborne debris, they now submit to the final indignity of dissolution crystal by crystal.

Preparing Planking, Gunwales, and Stems

With the planking stock piled ready for the saw, I am anticipating a productive day. If I am able to get the planking ready for pre-sanding, shortly after lunch I should also be able to make the gunwales and prepare the stems for the form. The white cedar planking stock is all an inch thick, and was bought rough as 3" and 6" boards 8-10' long; I will supplement it with a few 12-footers I have saved from an especially good lot. It has been air-drying now for about a year. The stock has been sorted for grain as well, and at least 80 percent of this batch is quarter-sawn, with the vertical grain ranging from tight-grained slow-growth wood with 25 or more lines to the inch, to fast-growth wood with as few as 8 or 10 lines per inch. I can use both types to good advantage in the canoe, along with a lesser amount of flat-grained planks as highlights in the less critical parts of the hull. I'll need two smooth edges on the planks in order to fit them together snuggly later, so before resawing the stock, I run it all past the table saw blade in two passes and end up with my standard-width stock 2-7/8" wide. The carbide blades that I favor not only give smooth results, but they are impervious to the silica and other minerals trapped in the porous cedar which can make this otherwise soft wood hard on regular blades.

I utilize the full capacity of the 10" blade in order to resaw the strips into thinner planking material, but the carbide blade and three-horsepower motor are up to the task. It can be argued that there would be less waste if I performed this step on my bandsaw using a skip-toothed blade, because the kerf of the blade (the wood turned into sawdust in the process) would be less than the 1/8" removed by the circular carbide blade. I'm more comfortable with the bench saw, however. It's the proper height for the job, and with the adequate horsepower I can feed the wood through faster. Also, the resulting planks are more uniform because the table saw blade is not as subject to the distortion common to all but the largest bandsaws put to such heavy use. Besides, the amount of wood I would save by using the skip-tooth blade is not enough to afford me a fourth strip from the 1" stock I commonly use. Still, don't hesitate to use your bandsaw for resawing if you prefer it, or want planking wider than 3", or if your home table saw isn't up to cutting 3" of material for hours on end.

I've had a good workout by the time I've resawn my pile into ¼"-thick stock. My planks average over 8-½' long, and I have 56 of them so I know I'll have plenty. If the quality wasn't so high, I would need extra to accommodate that lost to waste. Because of the resawing process, I am planking the whole canoe with stock starting from a pile that contained just 45 board feet of lumber.

My next step is to plane the stock to ⁵⁄₃₂" thickness and pile the bundle on a shelf by the drum sander for surface sanding in a day or two. Right now I am anxious to prepare the gunwales and stems, because it is beginning to look as though I will be able to bend the ribs over the form tomorrow.

I have some white spruce stock 20' long which is already ripped into rough gunwales just over an inch square. To rip long stock safely and accurately, it is necessary to utilize an off-cut table or rollers set up beyond the table for support of the emerging planks. Another roller set at the proper height 10' or so from the surface on the feed side is also advisable. Such an arrangment is in the interest of your own safety and the protection of the blade and the stock, and is preferable to using a helper to "catch" the wood as you feed it through. If you must resort to this tandem system, make sure the helper merely supports the wood as it emerges from the bench. You as the sawyer must do all the guiding and control the rate of the feed. If your stock isn't perfectly straight (and it seldom is), feed the saw with the slight bow rather than the arch against the fence. You should be able to work the piece through consistently in this manner — while it is impossible to force a sprung arc against the fence without binding the blade. A featherboard set up, is the best aid for insuring consistent results.

Inside gunwales may be square — ¹⁵⁄₁₆" would be about right for this standard 18' canoe, but traditionally they are a little deeper in dimension than they are wide; remember, the long, straight grain should be used for the top and bottom of the rail. The inwales I am preparing will be 1" deep and ⅞" wide, so I run them through the planer to get the desired size. On very light gunwales such as a "Featherweight" canoe, I reverse the proportions of the molding and siding, milling the gunwales so they actually end up wider than deep. This precaution is to keep the small-dimensioned gunwales from eventually losing their shape in the plan view by relaxing between the thwarts and causing hard spots. The inwales should sit in the canoe with their tops level across, rather than tilted in or out. If the model you choose to build has either tumblehome or flare, you will want to bevel your inwale accordingly on the rib side. First determine the average amount of tumblehome along the canoe's length; use this angle to set the saw for cutting the bevel. The exact amount of tumblehome will, no doubt, vary along the canoe, but if you try to match it locally, the top of your rail will vary in width. Start with a gunwale an inch square in dimension, and set the blade at the proper angle, so it will just touch the bottom outside edge, while removing the thick portion of the wedge along the top outside edge. On a flare-sided canoe, the wider surface rather than the narrower one will be uppermost in the canoe.

At this point, I pre-sand all the surfaces of the rails, except the rib side, by clamping them to a long bench and employing the belt sander equipped with a belt of 100 grit.

In all but the bluntest canoes, it is a nice touch to taper the ends of the gunwales in width where they run alongside the decks. It helps keep things light and graceful in appearance. Since the gunwales on the White canoe extend beyond the stem face (just as in the birchbark canoes), and the length of the deck is 16", I taper the final 18" of the inwales from full width down to ¼" at the tips after first cutting the rails to their exact length. The bandsaw works well for this job, once I've marked the taper clearly. I remove the meat from the rib side, to make it easier to fit the decks along the flat run on the inside later on. I like a smoothing plane for fairing the taper into the rest of the inwale.

Jig for prebending gunwales.

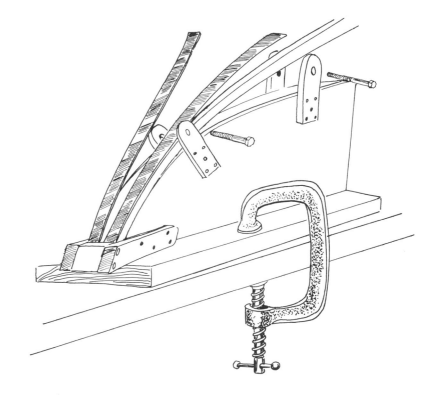

A long taper is cut onto the ends of the inwales and planed smooth.

A rasp is used to soften the edges of the stem notches. GC

Beveling the stem on the bandsaw. GC

The curved part of the stem must be beveled to match the run of the planking at the ends, and the straight portion is notched to receive the ribs that will be bent around it. To determine the location of the notches, remove the stems from the jig and place them on the form. The extra length at the butt will have to be marked and cut off, in order to fit the stem into the channel prepared for it on the form. Mark the locations of the metal bands on the stem, then use a cross section cut from a scrap rib to draw the shapes of the notches precisely. Remember that the notches are cut into the bottom and not the top surfaces of the stem, a point that can be confusing when working with the form in its upside down position. I use the bandsaw to cut the notches, then clean them up with a rasp, making sure the ribs will fit easily because they are going to swell slightly in the steam box.

The bevel along the stem curve is determined by the angle at which the planking, allowed to run naturally, would intersect it. In a canoe with a fine entry this will represent a shallow angle, 11 or 12 degrees, perhaps, while in a wide canoe with a blunt entry it may be closer to 18 or 20 degrees. Here again we must strike upon an average because to change it constantly would result in a stem face of varying widths. There is surprisingly little variance anyway, except down by the start of the curve, and here we must save room for the insertion of the cant ribs between the stem and garboard plank.

I mark the bevel and provide myself with guidelines for cutting it by first marking a $\frac{3}{8}$"-wide stem face at the top of the stem, then drawing the proper angle across the tip back toward the inside surface of the stem. These angle lines bisect the back or inside surface $\frac{1}{8}$" or so from the edge. Using my thumbnail as a gauge, I slide a pencil the whole length of the stem's inside surface down to the vicinity of the first notch, providing a clear line to guide the cut along once the table of the bandsaw is set at the proper angle. With a good sharp blade it is advisable to make the cuts without the use of a fence, which only makes it easier to bind the blade.

Start the cut with the stem face at the top end, flush against the table, and carefully push the stem past the blade along its curve, keeping the stem face flush at the blade at all times. This may take a little practice, so on your first attempt cut a little wide of your mark, making an allowance for some smoothing up with the spokeshave. As the first notch approaches the blade, gently lift the stem from the table as you continue to feed it, and the blade neatly and gradually exits the side of the stem.

If your bandsaw tilts in both directions, you will be able to reverse the tilt after completing one side of both stems, then finish the remaining sides in the same manner. My table tilts just one way sufficiently, so to cut the bevel on the second side of the stem, I must start the cut at the notch and cut along the curve to the tip. I begin by holding the face of the stem about an inch off the table at the notch, lowering it to the table as I advance the stem so that the blade takes an increasingly larger bite until it is cutting along my marked line with the stem flush on the surface. Then I follow the line out to the tip, just the opposite procedure I used for the other side. If you are not in a hurry, there is nothing that says that you can't use the spoke-shave to cut the bevels; I use mine now to clean up the bandsaw marks and for general smoothing, especially at the transition of the beveled portions into the sqaure butts. A thorough sanding with 80-grit paper now will make them ready to go on the form.

As a measure to conserve floorspace in my shop, I store the forms overhead on racks suspended from the beams. I have just enough time before supper to lower the 18' form onto sawhorses using a pair of blocks and tackle. With the shop vac I clean the accumulated dust from the form, sweep the floor, and call it a day.

April 17

My shop is in a one-time schoolhouse a half-mile up the road from our house. In decent weather it is a pleasant walk that affords me time to organize the day of building ahead. The rain continued through-out the night and I am not surprised the next morn-ing when I come across two crushed salamanders on the tarmac, one headed east when he met his fate, the other west. There are pools of meltwater lying in the woods east of the road, and my guess is that this morning there are clusters of jellylike eggs in some of them, deposited during a spawning frenzy by hundreds of writhing entangled creatures in the black of the forest night. But what of the two casu-alties on the road? The one facing west probably died sated and bleary, sapped by a primordial ecstacy as he contributed his genes to the icy incubator. The other, just as oblivious to the hazards of the crossing, was cut down unfulfilled, at the height of anticipation.

Bending the Ribs Into Place

The water in the buckets on the shop floor is unfrozen, and I fill the milking machine pail about half full and set it on the propane burner. Then I lower the steam box from its perch against the ceiling and set it squarely over the mouth of the steam chamber. While the water is heating up, I arrange the ribs in stacks according to height. Using a swatch of terrycloth tacked to a length of cedar, I drench each rib thoroughly front and back before setting it in its proper place in the steam box. This extra moisture keeps them from drying out in the steam box before I have a chance to use them all. I always arrange them in a pattern that makes it easy to identify the various lengths without fumbling while my head is enveloped in a cloud of steam. The top level of the box is always the hottest, so at one end I arrange the longest ribs on this level, because they will be the first to be bent, and at the other end the shortest because they must make the sharpest bends. By the time I drench and stick in the three leftover stems, clouds of vapor are starting to rise into the box.

I am lucky enough to have a helper today, a rare occurence which will certainly make my work easier. Together we clamp the gunwales in place on the form. The old form was equipped with hooks at each station which made it an easy matter to set the gunwales in place at the factory. When at some point the form was modified to eliminate the tumblehome, the hooks were never modified. I prefer the clamps anyway because I can put as many or few as I need, and place them precisely where they will do the most good. The stems are set in their slots on the form, held firmly by temporary wires, and the strongback with the various rib lengths marked upon it is bolted in place with just enough space beneath it to slide the ribs through. We are ready for bending about the same time the ribs are. To best determine this I pull one from the box, almost scorching my fingers, and flex it with both hands. I meet no resistance, so I know we can begin immediately.

Bending technique is important, but the process shouldn't be frightening. Once again care is the watchword. There is ample time before a rib cools off to place it properly on the form and execute the bend without rushing. This is a difficult point to impress upon beginners. They are usually so charged up with the excitement of their first wood-bending experience that they run around ineffectively at about twice normal speed, beads of sweat swelling on their brows, as they spasmodically bend the first few ribs. Fortunately after the initial panic, when they discover how easy it is, they usually settle down and concentrate on the few unhurried motions that yield the best results. Ribs should be stretched as they are pulled around the shape of

Wetting the ribs before placing them in the steam box. GC

Placing the ribs into the steam box in sequence. GC

The inwales are clamped firmly to the rail backer on the form. GC

The stem and gunwales temporarily joined on the form. GC

*(1-5) series Solo rib-bending technique.
all by GC*

   1. Bending the rib around the near side.
   *2. Reaching across form to bend the far
end.*
   3. Fastening the near end to the gunwale.
   4. Rebending and stretching the far end.
   *5. Fastening the second end. The
strongback keeps the ribs flush along the
bottom.*

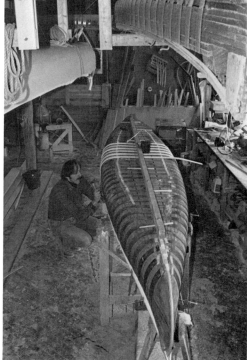

the form, because a casual bend will result in ribs that will loosen up as they cure on the form and cause problems later. When the rib has been slipped into its proper position beneath the strongback, place the palm of your hand firmly on the back of the rib between the strongback and the turn of the bilge, and grip the end with the other hand and pull it slowly around to conform to the metal band. A slight twisting action is required to make the leading edge of the frame sit snuggly against the metal. As much as it is possible, align the straight leading edge of the rib with the edge of the metal band in order to achieve uniform spacing. Occasionally you will encounter a stubborn rib that will have to be displaced slightly from this pattern in order to get it to lie flat, but with adequately steamed ribs you can generally make them conform. When the bend is completed and the rib touches the gunwale, relax it about halfway and stretch it around again, repeating this two or three times before finally nailing the rib to the rail with two ring nails spaced between the ribs edges and centerline, about in the middle of the inwale.

The first rib pulled from the box breaks when we try bending amidships, but it was a problem with the grain that caused the failure rather than insufficient exposure to the steam, and we do one entire end of the canoe without breaking another. At the stem we hold the rib firmly in the notch and bend the ends slowly around. Once nailed at the gunwale, we add another slightly shorter ring nail through the rib and into the stem at the notch after predrilling a small pilot hole. The final rib at the end must be folded almost in two, the bend is so sharp, and to increase our chances of success we first bend it over the preceding rib, then move it ahead to its own notch and bend it again; this time with good results. A few stray torn fibers sticking up from the sharp bend are acceptable, and these will be shaved off before planking. Actual breaks in the rib, however, or separations of large layers of the grain pattern will require replacements.

We proceed down the opposite end of the form, with everything continuing to run smoothly. As we complete a section, I tighten down the bolt pressing the center of the ribs flush against the form.

We finish the job in about an hour and a quarter, breaking three ribs during the whole operation, which is about average. Still it is nice to have the cushion of a few extras left in the box, and they will never go to waste. I give the stem stock an extra 15 minutes in the box with the doors closed before trying to bend one. The second snaps, and when I release the batten, a big sliver peels off eventually slicing the stem in two. But the last piece holds, and the jig is once again filled to capacity.

A new canoe is being born over the core of the ancient form. Its delicate symmetrical skeleton is already formed; the pattern of the bright new wood stands out smartly against the dark worn strips beneath. It could as well be the skeletal system of a marine creature, and indeed there are parallels. But the real life of this swimmer belongs to the past, when on some ridge above a swamp the vigorous cedar trees were year by year growing new layers of straight, sound wood. The future "life" is imparted by the builder's care and skill. His attention to detail will determine whether the finer elements sought by the designer will be fully realized, or buried by compromise.

The ribs will have to be faired one to another before I can begin planking, but I'll let them dry overnight before disturbing them. After fairing, I'll wait another day or two before planking to ensure that the ribs are fully cured to their new shapes. The ribs have a tendency to round out on the bottoms of canoes that are hurried off the form; and although I don't want a dead-flat bottom on this canoe, I don't care for a perfectly round one either. When it can be arranged, I'll bend my ribs on a Friday, let them sit over the weekend, fair Monday, and plank Tuesday and Wednesday. Thursday morning, after more than five days on the form, the hull is ready to be lifted free.

There is enough left of the day to make the half ribs I plan to install in the canoe, and since I'll be setting up for the job, I will mill enough blanks for eight or ten batches. Half ribs are placed along the bottom of the canoe between the regular ribs. They diminish in length towards the ends of the canoe, reaching across the bottom from bilge to bilge. Their function is twofold; they add strength to the canoe's bottom without eliminating the natural resilience, and together with the ribs, form an almost solid floor which protects the planking from gear which might otherwise slip in between the regular ribs. In some regions half ribs are referred to as "walking ribs," because they afford the poler a secure platform when he is standing in the canoe, and even walking up and down in it to change the trim.

In the center of the canoe, the half ribs are the same thickness as the ribs — 5/16″ — but thinned to about 3/16″ or less at the ends. This keeps the ends supple so they don't distort the planking when they end near a planking seam. The half ribs in this 18′6″ canoe range in length from 30″ amidships to 14″ at the stems, the lengths predetermined to result in a pleasing pattern in the bottom of the canoe.

I've been saving rib stock cut-offs to make the half ribs from, and these run 18″ to 36″ long, 2-1/4″ wide, and as thick as the ribs. I first pre-sand the best surface, then, on the bench saw, split them exactly in half lengthwise — ending up with stock just under 1-1/8″ wide.

My router is still set up for shaping the edges of the ribs, so by adding a featherboard, I can run a continuous chain of the half rib stock through for shaping very quickly, and before I know it I have enough half rib stock for several canoes ready to be cut to length and thinned. I save out enough for the current project, and store the rest under a bench.

Referring to my list, I first cut the blanks to the proper lengths — marking them accordingly on the back side — then take them over to the drum sander where I thin the ends. The taper at the ends is 8-9″ long on the longer ribs and perhaps 5″ on the short ones, and again, the meat is removed from the backside. I've gotten pretty good at making fair, even tapers without a trace of a hollow by holding

All the ribs bent onto the form.

Tapering the ends of the half ribs on the drum sander.

the stock against the drum at the start of the taper and working gradually toward the ends in one slow motion. It has taken a while to perfect this technique, however, so some practice is in order for beginners. I also round and bevel the tips to match the shaping on the sides. A little hand-sanding to remove the hairs left along the edges by the drum sander, and I am finished with them until I am ready to put them on the form later tomorrow.

Visitors to my rather isolated, unmarked shop are rare, but the dogs are barking wildly at the door shaking their tails, so I know someone is out there now. It's an older fellow from a nearby town who stops in once in awhile to see what projects are underway and to tell me about his neighbor who built canoes in Milo years ago. It is a welcome reprieve and will save me from cutting and shaping the decks today.

April 18th

On my walk to the shop today I intercepted a muskrat stealing across the road towards the pond, and was glad not to have the dogs along for company. "Musquash," Thoreau called them after the Indian fashion, and I like that term better. Sensing danger, she picked up her hurried pace, her head down and beady eyes on the path ahead. Frail she looked after the long winter, not sleek in the least as she tiptoed along on her skinny black feet. Her back hunched slightly as she scuttled along, dragging her eel-like tail behind, her route anything but a straight line. It was a dull, puzzled look she gave me when I momentarily cut her off, but her bewhiskered rodent muzzle was not without its peculiar charms. Too busy to chat, she dodged to the left and continued on her purposeful way.

The Last of the Ribs, Then Decks and Thwarts

Today it is my intention to fair the ribs, install the half ribs onto the form, and make the decks and thwarts. It is all within reason, and if realized will provide me with the opportunity to begin planking tomorrow, which is Friday.

The old White form is reasonably fair, but even though we were careful in our bending, the ribs can stand a little adjustment and a good going over with the fairing block so the planking will sit flush on each frame. Working on a quarter of the canoe at a time, I check the ribs one to another with a 3' section of planking, holding it as flat as possible in the configuration it will later be attached. It shows me graphically if there is a lifted edge or a bulging rib that was not stretched adequately and is now loose. I can resolve most discrepancies by rocking the rib a little forward, so that it sits better on the band, or pulling it back slightly to flatten a high trailing edge. Once in a while I have to remove nails in the gunwales and move the end of a rib slightly forward or back. Normally, the whole center section is perfect, and these fine adjustments take place near the ends. I use the spokeshave conservatively on a couple of ribs up by the stem to knock off a little shoulder to one side of the notches. Once I am satisfied with one entire side of the canoe, I take my fairing block and begin sanding the outside surface of the ribs fair to one another. My block is made from 3"-square cedar stock about 20" long. The ends curve up so the thing doesn't catch when I'm using it across the ribs. Attached to it is a half-sheet of 40-grit paper made for a floor-sanding machine.

I first work the block across the ribs, in a back-and-forth motion, each stroke treating a section of five or six ribs at the minimum. I spend a lot of time in the stem area, making sure the ribs at this critical entry region are fair in all respects. The sanding marks are visible the full width of all the ribs being worked, so I know they are pretty much in line, and move on to another section. A lot of fine dust is generated by this process, but the amount of wood being removed is negligible and the step essential to ensure the planking sits snuggly against all the ribs. I use my scrap piece of planking to check frequently, and when I am satisfied I then pull the block laterally along the ribs from strongback to gunwale in overlapping sections to remove any ridges created by the longitudinal fairing. When one

Fairing the ribs with the fairing block.

side is finished, I repeat the procedure on the opposite, then remove the strongback temporarily without disturbing the relative positions of the ribs. I fair the center portions of the ribs by using the block along the ribs only. With the strongback removed, any action across the ribs would be sure to knock some of them out of place and defeat the careful work I've already completed. I remove the dust with my shop vac, then replace the strongback and tighten it down.

I've had water heating in the milking pail while I finished up the fairing; now it's at a rolling boil and time to put the half ribs in on end for softening. The form has metal strips for the half ribs just as it does for the frames, and near each end is a cleverly bent nail, its head on the inside of the form; it can be raised from its latent position against the form, and turned to hold the end of a half rib in place. The metal strips are the proper lengths, so it's a simple matter for me to pick one or two of the longer half ribs from the water, slide them one at a time beneath the strongback, justify the ends with those of the metal bands beneath, and lock them in place with the bent nails. I pay attention to the spacing of the half ribs between the ribs as well, keeping everything as even as possible. Each time I take the two longest ribs from the water for installation, I turn the remaining ones over so both ends get a good soaking in the hot water. There is little bend to those amidships, so I can start immediately. By the time I get to the tighter bends near the ends, the shorter half ribs will have had time to soak adequately. I get all the half ribs on in less than an hour, except for five where the strongback bolts prevent their installation until the hull is removed from the form. As long as I take care not to displace any of them when I

The half ribs in place. GC

The ends of the half ribs are held in place by the bent nails.

begin planking, I will have a very satisfactory job, and will have improved the strength of the canoe significantly, while adding very little weight.

I can scarcely believe a second visitor in as many days. This one, however, is selling industrial supplies, principally for machine shops, and I can tell at a glance there is nothing among his wares that I can't do without. He is soon on his way and I on mine to make some decks for the canoe. I have a lovely piece of mahogany set aside for the purpose, and since it will nicely match the stock I expect to use for the outwales, I take down my deck patterns and begin. I prefer good flat-grained stock for my decks. It is attractive, and I can usually select a grain pattern that enhances not only the appearance, but also the strength of the decks. Most canoe decks are large enough proportionately so it is unnecessary to find stock with grain that exactly conforms to the shape, as with some boat breasthooks that are drawn into elongated tangs on each side. In the typical canoe, only the poorest quality wood would ever result in deck failure, so it is largely a matter of aesthetics. If you have been saving that perfect piece of hardwood, now is the time to bring it out of storage, and if you enjoy laminating up attractive patterns of wood, perhaps with a cross-shaped spline in the center for accent, here's your chance to add an individual touch.

After planing the stock to 1", I cut out the shapes on the bandsaw, just barely leaving the line. Holding the rough decks in the vise I work the edges smooth, exactly to the line with the spokeshave. There is a slight hollow to the shape of the decks in plan view, and I am careful not to eliminate that as I work. Using a section of ribstock to represent the gunwale, I check each edge to make sure there will be no gaps once the deck is in place. A canoe with tumblehome in the ends requires beveled edges on the decks, the top surface slightly smaller than the bottom. A flared bow requires the opposite bevel for a proper fit. When I am satisfied with the edges, I concentrate on smoothing the end curve of the decks with a rasp and sandpaper. The bottom surface of the deck at the wide end is hollowed out with a gouge, to a kind of inverted crescent that adds to the fineness of the appearance of the bow.

My next step is marking the decks for crowning. It doesn't take much of a camber to improve the appearance over the flat variety; too much, however, can impart a woody appearance — just the opposite of what we are trying to achieve. I draw a line ⅛" from the top, the length of the deck on both edges, and carve the crown from this modest excess. The decks are held firmly in place on the bench in a little holder: simply two ¼"-square sections of

Cutting out the decks on the bandsaw

A gouge is used to hollow out the underside of the decks.

Carving the deck's crown with the spokeshave.

The finished decks.

cedar nailed to the bench in the shape of the deck's outline. To begin, I cut a bevel on each side down to my line with a small plane. Then using the spokeshave, I gradually work it into a fair crown that extends evenly across the width of the deck. It is obviously a shallower crown at the wider portion of the deck than at the point. I smooth the deck with 60-grit sandpaper before setting it aside for later installation in the canoe.

Thwarts are frequently bulkier and thicker than they need to be, and since these are hardwood members, add unnecessary weight to the finished product. The thin, sculptured thwarts of the Indian birch canoes have proven adequate for their work over the ages and indicate to me what proportions are satisfactory. The center thwart must be strong enough to bear the weight of the entire canoe when it is being carried by a single person, and since the process of getting the canoe onto one's shoulders is not always a smooth action (it can be with a little practice), the strain put on the thwart is momentarily magnified. Still, the average center thwart (and almost all quarter thwarts found in factory produced canoes) is much beefier than necessary, and would benefit by a little careful whittling. I like to install a simple yoke amidships, which distributes the weight a little more evenly across the collarbones and neck vertebrae, and makes it easier to balance the canoe. Pads made from a square of plywood and several layers of closed-cell foam, neatly wrapped in canvas or leather, may be fashioned to bolt onto such a yoke, and used wherever portaging becomes a serious matter, such as in the Boundary Waters Canoe Area of Minnesota, and the adjacent Quetico.

White ash has the ideal amounts of strength and spring for thwarts and yokes, and I start by planing the stock down to ¾". Thwarts with flat grain look best, and it is not a requirement to use quarter-sawn lumber for this purpose. I take down my patterns for a center yoke, quarter thwarts, and the little end thwarts and draw out all five shapes on the stock, taking best advantage of grain and color to enhance the thwarts' appearance in the canoe.

Once again I cut just outside the lines, affording myself the opportunity to shave precisely to the the line with the spokeshave to fair the outlines before I begin shaping them. Once they are fair, I run them by the table-mounted router which is equipped with a radius bit with a little roller-bearing guide. I end the radius where the neck of the thwart widens back out to full width, leaving the crisp corner along the short straight run at the end of the thwart. I was once content to work with these molded thwarts on the drum sander to achieve the final shaping, but now I work down the surfaces further with the spokeshave until the cross section of the thwart is more elliptical than oval. I take more wood off the quarter thwarts than I do the straight portions of the yoke. Using a rasp, I work down the inside surface of the yoke's center to make it as comfortable as possible. Only when I am satisfied that I have removed as much wood as possible without sacrificing the required strength, do I smooth them up on the drum sander. Finally a good going over with regular sandpaper, first 60 then 80 grit, prepares the thwarts for future installation.

I've worked a bit overtime today, but with the spring sunshine flooding the shop through the south-facing windows, and my goal of planking tomorrow within easy reach, I certainly was not even aware that the 5 pm whistle had sounded in workplaces across the land, nearly an hour before my work was completed.

A molded yoke can be sustituted for the center thwart, and facilitates solo carrying. GC

April 19th

It has been an easy winter for the deer by this region's standards. The snow seldom exceeded 18" in the woods and was rarely anywhere near that deep. Prolonged periods of subzero temperatures were also scarce and the deer were mobile all winter long, foraging throughout their range instead of being hemmed into their yarding areas, where beset by deep drifts and vicious cold, they customarily wait out the worst part of the lean season.

On my way to the store for milk at dusk last evening, I spotted along the far edge of a field, seven light, horizontal forms, moving like spectres against the dark woods behind. The field had been planted to alfalfa years ago, and clusters of the cloverlike legume still hold out against the more vigorous coarse grasses. Now that the snow has melted, the deer are cropping the withered but still tasty tops, building up their strength for the fawning season ahead. As I slowed the car, they scarcely noticed; but when I stopped completely their heads came up and their ears cocked slightly forward. Not wishing to interrupt them in their important work, I elected to be a good neighbor and slowly drove along to my business.

Planking

Planking is the most fun and also one of the most critical steps in the canoe-building process. The relative speed with which the hull develops during this step can be truly gratifying, but the task should never be hurried and careful attention to detail is in order.

In most traditional wooden boats, each plank is tapered to match the wide and narrow sections of the hull. Most of these planking patterns are derived by mathematically dividing the girth of the boat at its various stations by the number of strakes that will be used to plank it, although a really attractive planking job by a skilled builder takes a few other factors into consideration. The planking on a wood-canvas canoe departs from this tradition for a number of reasons, foremost being economy of time and materials. Because the planking stock is so thin and flexible, it is possible to twist it into tight spots that would be impossible with more conventional stock. This allows you as the builder to attach a large portion of the planking along the bottom of the canoe, using full-width stock with little or no shaping. It is easy to see how this can save time, but it also saves material when you consider that shaped planks on conventional boats must be cut from wider stock, resulting in a fair amount of waste. This was an important factor to canoe manufacturers who were producing hundreds of canoes to be sold at very competitive prices. It is important to you today, because good-quality planking stock is both expensive and in short supply. The differences in girth because of the canoe's shape are eventually resolved by the goring strakes — a few tapered planks along the bilge area of the hull. A neat goring job can be very attractive, and if the planks are carefully selected it actually enhances the appearance of the hull. Still, some people object to this shortcut method of planking, and if you are one of them, you may wish to work out your proportions for tapering all the planks. Keep in mind, though, that the canvas skin will be covering most of your efforts, and that on the inside of the hull a neat goring job looks just as pleasing as the alternate method.

Before I put on a single plank, I sort out all the material for grain pattern and color. This makes it easy to select matching sections which from the inside will give the appearance that the canoe was planked with full-length stock, which is far from the case. While water is heating on my burner, I remove the bolts from the strongback, place it just to one side of the centerline, and brace it down firmly against the ribs from the overhead with sections of 2x2. The strongback is still required to hold the ribs flat against the metal bands on the bottom, but I don't want bolt holes in the planking that will eventually have to be patched. Many factories actually bolted the strongbacks down through the planking, however, and the neatly matched sections that were patched in were scarcely noticeable and seemed not to cause any problems structurally.

I spring a chalkline next to the strongback from stem to stem, representing the centerline of the canoe, and pick out the stock for my first garboard plank. The garboard plank runs flat along the canoe's bottom then must twist nearly 90 degrees to conform to the plane of the stem. It is asking much of any material, and I always select some quarter-sawn stock with relatively wide spacing between the straight lines of the grain. Here I am using some of my longer stock and making a single butt joint a couple ribs from center. To ensure a square cut, I first mark the butts with a combination square, then cut overlapping 45-degree bevels with the utility knife, using a straight scrap of hardwood for a cutting guide. Next I attach the plank lightly to every third or fourth rib by driving one of the $^{11}/_{16}''$ tacks through the center of the plank and rib alike. It clinches into the wood on the inside when it strikes the metal band beneath. I use a seven-ounce casement hammer, which is far preferable to a clumsy, heavy framing model for this use. Once I have the full length of the strake laid out in this manner, I soak my terricloth swab in the

The tacking pattern amidships. Note the extra tacks at the butt joint and the fastening of the half ribs. GC

pail of hot water and liberally douse both ends of the garboard to soften them for the big twist. I give the cedar time to absorb the water while I drive all the nails along the bottom. If you've examined many old canoe hulls, you've noticed there are variations in the tacking patterns. In my experience, the most effective is a pattern of three tacks placed diagonally across the plank. On the right-hand end of the canoe as it is planked, the top tack is in the upper left-hand corner of the junction of plank and rib, another placed in the center of the junction, and the third in the lower right-hand corner. It is just the opposite pattern on the left-hand end of the canoe. This pattern provides the maximum holding power where the edges tend to lift as the plank is rolled down around the shoulder or turn of the bilge. It is also a neat pattern and requires fewer extra tacks to hold everything down snuggly. With any pattern, avoid placing tacks closer than $1/8$" from the planking edge, and $1/4$" from the edges of the ribs. Trying for too wide a pattern will result in splits along the beveled edges of the ribs and much fussing to correct the damage.

With the garbord plank attached along the bottom I can concentrate on one of the ends. After rewetting it I secure the top edge of the plank to the stem, using two 18-gauge steel wire nails between ribs and a single, 14-gauge bronze nail where the ribs cross the stem. Then, after drenching the plank a third time I carefully roll the plank down, nailing it at each rib as I work toward the end until it conforms to the sharply bent ribs at the end of the form. Hurrying this step will only lead to a split garboard. Be sure to use plenty of hot water and a firm and steady hand when executing this twist. I next fasten the lower edge of the plank to the stem where it runs by, trim the excess to

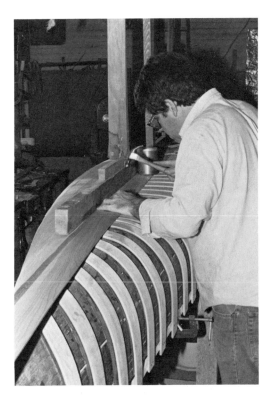

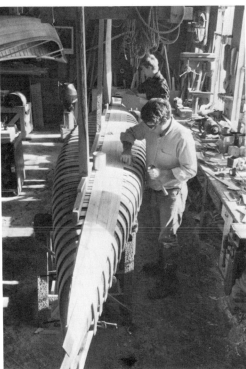

The wetted garboard plank folded around the entry. Subsequent planks are not fastened to the stem until the canoe comes off the form. GC

Nailing a plank to the ribs. GC

Planking the hull. GC

match the curve of the stem, and fasten it along this curve with several more wire nails. I treat the other end in a similar manner, again without splitting the plank during the critical twist.

I select three matching planking sections which will make up my second course. This is a good place to use the very tightest vertical-grained planks, because they will be highly visible in the bottom of the canoe and the twists in this part of the boat are more moderate than at the turn of the bilge. Again, I lay out the whole strake, lightly tacking the sections in place, then I swab hot water onto the portions that will be bent around the quarters of the canoe. I fasten the planks, starting from the center of the canoe and working toward the ends. Occasionally, a plank will need a little fitting near the ends; this I accomplish by shaving any excess off the edge with a finger plane. Normally on this model, the planking fits without fussing and there are no wedge-shaped gaps at the ends that must be filled in later. On some designs, it is impossible to get all the planking at the ends to come together without excessive edge-setting. You are allowed to force the planks lightly to make them fit, but too much force can cause the planking to buckle — if not immediately, then later on. It is preferable to fashion small wedges of planking to fill these end gaps once the canoe is taken off the form. This and all subsequent strakes are allowed to run by the stem without fastening; otherwise it would be impossible to remove the hull from the form later on.

The third, fourth, and fifth strakes are attached the same way. I like to stagger my butt joints as far apart as possible, and continue with my nailing pattern, with an occasional extra tack driven wherever it will help hold down a lifted edge. The planking is fastened to the half ribs as well, and I am careful to unhook the nails holding the half ribs in place, pushing them down out of my way before I bury them with the next course of planking. A large portion of the planking is wetted as I lay it down, especially that which has to cup around the turn of the bilge. This wetting causes the planks to swell slightly in width (other varieties of wood swell an even greater amount), so I fit the wet planking one to another as tightly as I can. As the planking dries out over the next few days, fine planking seams will become apparent, and these small gaps will accommodate the natural swelling that will occur when the canoe is used or stored where it will be subject to the prevailing humidity. Without this built-in leeway, the planks would buckle whenever the canoe was used in very moist or wet conditions. Our friends in Sweden, who use spruce to plank their canoes, deliberately leave even spaces between courses to

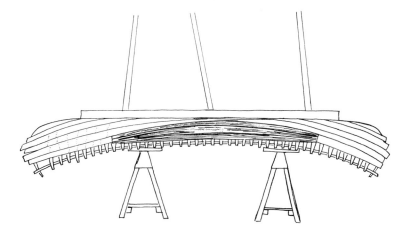

Tapered or gored planks.

allow for this later expansion. With our very stable white cedar this practice is not necessary, however, especially when a large percentage of the stock is quarter sawn.

With five full-width planks attached, it becomes obvious that I will have to do something to address the great differences in girth along the length of the canoe. My fifth strake comes within 6″ of the sheer near the ends, but amidships there is a 1′-wide gap between the planking and the rail. It is also obvious from the resistance I encountered twisting the final plank into place that I cannot simply continue nailing one full-width plank after another. It is clearly time for the goring. Each canoe model will have a unique goring pattern that best meets the requirements. Since I've built this canoe many times I don't even have to think about it; but you will when you build your first canoe, so here are some of the points you should consider. Your objective is to fill in the wide-bellied shape left to be planked, using tapered planks that will look as even and symmetrical as possible. The goring planks must be allowed to lie as naturally as possible, to eliminate edge-setting that can later cause buckling between the ribs. The goring will span the portion of the canoe from amidships to the shallow section just before the sheerline starts to rise sharply — usually rib six to nine from the stem. You may allow the planks to run out to a feather edge but this is less desirable than bringing them to a joint with another full-width plank in the quarters.

On my form the distance between rib number eight at one end to the corresponding rib at the other is about 10′. When I attach at plank to the center rib and let it run naturally toward each end, the bottom edge runs by rib eight about an inch below the full-width plank above. By tapering or goring the plank from its full width amidships to 1″ at the end, I can get a nice fit and will have picked up 2

Device for marking goring.

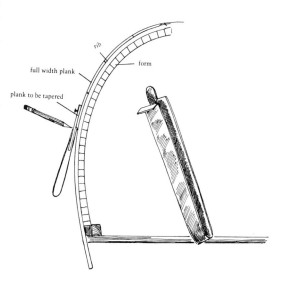

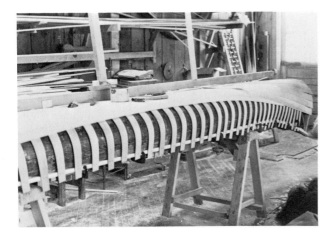

The area to be gored.

Using a marking device to mark the taper or gore. GC

of the 6″ I must make up on this side of the canoe. I've become quite proficient at this tapering business, which used to be quite a mysterious art; but now I use a little marking gauge, one that allows first-timers to gore the planks essentially as well as I could by eye after years of practice, and the device has speeded up the process for me, too. It was given to me by Howard Spinney of Old Town, who used to work at the White Canoe factory back when wooden canoes were still being produced there. I fasten the plank firmly at the center and tack it lightly at each end where it crosses rib eight. The gauge looks something like a pair of ice cube tongs, and the inside tang is inserted beneath the goring plank, at each rib and pushed up until the little lip at the top rests against the plank above. The top edge of the outside tang corresponds to the inside lip, and by drawing a mark along the edge on the plank to be gored, I have a visual point at each rib, indicating how much wood will have to come off for a good fit. Once I've marked the gore, I remove the tack from the end of the plank, and with the utility knife, cut away the wood to within ⅛″ or so of the marks. I take it down even closer with the finger plane, fairing the curve as I work toward the end. For indeed, the taper has a definite crown to it and is not a straight line which can be precut on the bench. Finally I carefully fit the gored plank from center toward the end, removing small amounts of wood from the high spots until I am satisfied with the fit. I bevel the edge slightly to the inside along the rather sharply curved bilge area. The amount of cupping required by this first goring plank in order to fit around the tightest part of the bilge is nothing short of extraordinary, and I apply plenty of hot water to keep the wood from splitting. Once one end of the plank is fit and fastened, I treat the other in the same fashion.

I've marked the width of a full plank on rib eight, and roughly divided the distance into thirds, because my inten-

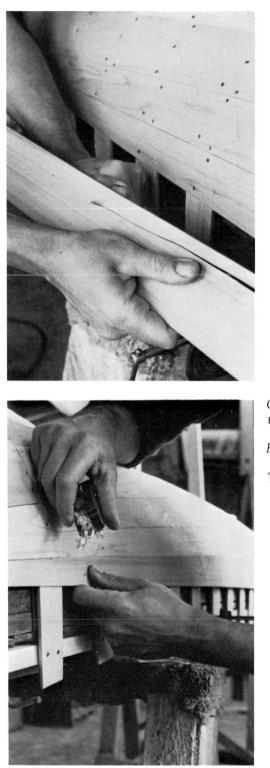

Cutting down to the marks with the utility knife. GC

Fitting the gore with a small plane. GC

The fit completed. GC

Gored planks (four in this instance) taper to a neat joint with a single full-width plank in the quarters.

tion is to make my three goring strakes mesh exactly with a full-width plank at this point. This means that I may have to slightly influence the runs of the second and third gores, but I will avoid heavy edge-setting. Because I've perfected this pattern over the course of building many canoes, I'm confident that it will come out about right.

After lunch I fit the final goring plank on side one, then attach the end planks into which the tapers converge. There is a gap remaining that is almost a single plank in width, between the last gore and the sheer, but this sheer-strake is best fit when the canoe is off the form, and I've come to the end of the metal bands on the form anyway. I slide the strongback over onto the garboard plank, brace it down, and begin planking the other side by carefully attaching the second garboard. Because the framing structure of the canoe is held rigid on the form, it is possible to plank just one side at a time. On a regular small boat, built over molds and held together by ribbands, it is necessary to plank the two sides simultaneously to even out the stresses and prevent the hull from twisting or otherwise distorting.

By now I am really into the rhythm that always develops when I'm planking a canoe — the selection of complementary planks, cutting and fitting them, and then driving the tacks home; quitting time catches me by surprise with two final goring strakes to be fit. It is the weekend, and we'll be out of town. The nearly planked hull will benefit by another two days on the form, and I can look forward to Monday when I'll get the first look at my handiwork on the all-important interior of the canoe.

April 22

The mating flight of the male woodcock is something to behold. It seems an excessively demonstrative measure if it is all merely to attract the mottled, long-billed hens. Sunday evening they were thick above the shrinking fields of an abandoned farm, so reckless in their descents we half-expected to find them impaled in the earth by their bills, quivering like so many lawn darts. The air was permeated with a medley of the sounds accompanying this ritual — a symphony of electronic breeps, coarse twitterings, and crystal clear little melodies interlaced as several birds took to the nighttime sky at once.

The ascending spirals remain most fascinating to me. Beginning conservatively, the woodcock's flight uncoils into wider and wider loops, the higher he climbs into the thickening dusk. The black dot of his body diminishes steadily, then disappears altogether. One hopes against all reason that this unraveling pattern is perhaps the formula for defying gravity, and that the lovestruck bird has emerged above the stratosphere. But then the song changes, and its alarmingly clear that the forces of gravity have regrouped and are violently reclaiming the fugitive, plummeting the little ball of feathers swiftly towards the earth, where only a last-second maneuver by the little aerobat prevents a violent and messy impact.

Tying Together the Deck, Inwales, and Stem

By 9:30 I've finished the final goring strakes, just in time to catch Rollin on his way to Bangor, and get him to help me lift the hull from the form. I've removed the C-clamps and the little wires that hold the ends of the stems in place. With two people it is an easy matter to free the gunwales from the slots by pushing down on the hull and gently pulling them free section by section. Even after several days on the form, the ribs are springy enough to spread the canoe sufficiently. If the reasons for not attaching the ends of the planking to the stems while the canoe was on the form were not apparent earlier, you will appreciate them now.

Once the boat is off the form, I set it on a pair of horses and temporarily pull it into shape with three braces designed to fit over the gunwales amidships and near the ends, to hold the canoe roughly in shape. An examination

The hull lifted from the form.

Releasing the planked hull from the form. GC

The hull is temporarily held in shape by spacers. GC

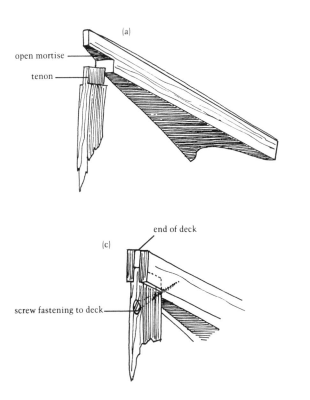

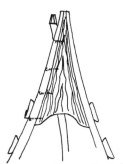

(b) gunwales screwed to deck,
stem off to one side

Installing a deck without the gunwales running by.

of the interior reveals a satisfactory planking job, but one rib and one half rib were split badly during the planking process and will have to be replaced.

There are various methods of tying together the deck, inwales, and stem, and I like to think my system is one of the better ones. Many early builders simply ran the stem up past the nibbed-off deck and drove a screw through to hold it together. Others would end the stem beneath the deck and actually sink a screw down through the deck into the fragile top of the stem. It is a small wonder most old canoes exhibit serious deterioration in this area.

Later on a few companies — including Old Town —improved the method of joining these members when they began cutting out a notch on the underside of the deck and fashioning a tenon at the tip of the stem which fit into the notch. A screw was still necessary to keep the stem from escaping out the forward end of the notch, however.

On the old White canoes the gunwales ran past the stem with the ends joined beyond the stemface, just as in a birch canoe. These extended inwales, coupled with a notch on the underside of the deck, form an ideal mortise arrangement for a tenon cut on the top of the stem, which eliminates entirely the requirement for a screw. The White factory never took advantage of this possibility, and simply ran the stems up past the decks, covering the whole business with a brass cap; I prefer blending the two methods to get a sturdy, fastener-free joint.

The tenon at the tip of the stem fits into a mortise cut in the underside of the deck. Here the inwales run past the stem completing the mortise.

My first step is to mark lines across the stem indicating where the inwales intersect. Because everything has relaxed somewhat since the canoe came off the form, I force the rails upwards and draw the stem back a bit, mark the stem where the gunwales cross it top and bottom, then saw the end of the stem off midway between the two marks. On the new stem top I trace the shape of the deck near the tip, leaving a 1/8" space on either side of the deck. The very point of the deck runs past the stem about 3/8". The 1/8" space on either side of the tenon will become a little shoulder on which the gunwales will rest.

I then carefully mark the tenon using these reference marks, and with a fine-toothed Japanese saw and chisel cut and clean up the tenon. The corresponding notch is marked on the deck. I derive the length of the notch by setting the deck on the top of the tenon and marking it at the back of the stem. To get the proper depth, I hold the deck in place against the inwale and bring the stem alongside. The top of the tenon represents the maximum depth of the notch. Once the elongated notch is cut, the deck is ready to attach to the inwale. I lightly butter the edge of the deck with a marine bedding compound as a sealer and screw one side to the inwale using four 1-1/2" No. 8 bronze wood screws. Before I can bring the remaining inwale alongside, I must shave off part of the inwale that extends past the deck so the two rails will slide past one another. Then, using a bar clamp, I draw the other gunwale and deck together. I have marked the gunwales near the ends, to indicate their relative positions when they were on the form. Now I line up these markes and hold the stem temporarily in place, I check the relative position of everything. The deck appears to be sitting level and the stem plumb. I check my observations by running a string up to the tip of the deck from the base of the stem at the far end of the canoe. There is a centerline marked on the middle brace and I try to align optically the taut string, the centerline mark on the brace, and the seam between my two garboard planks. At this point the stem is held out of the way off to one side by the gunwale. If something is askew it is impossible to get the string to run by the brace at the centerline when everything else lines up. Adjustments are made by sliding the unfastened gunwale forward or back along the deck, thus altering the relative heights of the rails. If this check confirms my initial alignment, the second gunwale is fastened to the deck. The ends of the gunwales are fastened together beyond the decks with small screws, and the stem top is forced permanently into its notch.

Small things like moving the stem during the rib-bending process, or pulling the curve of the stem slightly out of center when nailing on the garboard can make it tricky getting all the parts together while keeping the stem straight. If you are careful, and align everything as closely as possible during the deck installation, your stems should be plumb for all appearances and purposes.

As soon as both decks are installed, I cut down the projecting ends of the ribs to within 1/8" of the gunwale surface with the sabersaw, then fit a 3/16" bit into the chuck of the electric drill in preparation for installing the yoke and thwarts. The gunwales and thwarts are drilled in place because there is no satisfactory way of aligning the two separately. A good method is to use bar clamp to bring the hull together snuggly against the ends of the thwarts. Be careful — too much pressure here can cause the thwarts to buckle, or more likely force the ribs to separate from the gunwales. The flat top of the thwart should be perfectly flush against the bottom surface of the gunwale. With everything held in place, it is a simple matter to support one end of the thwart or yoke with one hand while drilling the bolt hole with the other. Care should be taken to keep the end of the thwart centered on the rib, and the bolt hole centered on the gunwales as well as on the end of the thwart below. For a while I was unable to purchase bronze carriage bolts less than 1/4" in diameter, and because I feared weakening the gunwales excessively, I used only one bolt at each end of the center thwart or yoke when two would have been better. A pair of bolts at each end prevents the thwart from twisting or rocking when the canoe is being lifted and portaged, eliminating most of the wear on bolt holes which can result in gunwale failure years later. Now that 3/16" carriage bolts are again available, thanks to Rollin

Placement of thwart bolts.

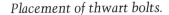
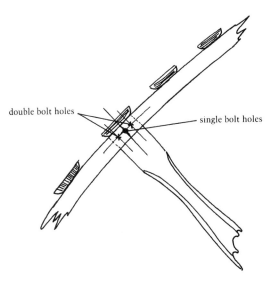

double bolt holes

single bolt holes

ordering a huge amount from a manufacturer, I use two bolts and center them between the centerline of the thwart and the edges. A single bolt, however, is adequate for each end of the quarter thwarts.

With the decks and thwarts in place, the canoe should assume its intended fair shape in both profile and plan views. If it does not, and hard spots are obvious along the sheerline, something is wrong with either the length or placement of the thwarts, the rise of the sheer, or the shape of the decks; you will have to trace these possibilities down one by one if you hope to improve things.

I have just time enough left before lunch to nail the planking ends to the stems. I use 18-gauge steel wire nails for the purpose, 5/8″ long, five to a plank. Bronze nails of the same size would of course be better, but the smallest available are 15 gauge and these are too large when you consider the number of fastenings the stem will receive before the canoe is completed. Brass escutcheon pins are available in the proper length and gauge, but the tiny heads are inadequate for the job; cut tacks, designed for clinching, would work themselves out in time because of their wedge shape. The steel nails in the factory canoes seemed to work satisfactorily in this application over the years.

I place the nails close to the backside of the stem, angling them slightly forward to hold the panks flush against the whole width of the beveled side. I like doing this step with the hull upside down on the horses, and I back up the stem with the clinching iron as I drive the nails. I alternate sides as I nail planks to the stem from the garboards toward the deck, minimizing the risk of pulling or twisting the stem out of alignment during the process. As each plank is fastened, I cut it to length at the very face of the stem.

The planking at the ends of the canoe between the stems and the last bent ribs will need the support of two pairs of cant ribs. These are not bent around the stem, but instead fit between the garboard and stem on opposite sides. I match and fit them as carefully as possible, and most people are fooled into believing they are actully one-piece members.

To begin, I plane two ribs down to 1/4″ in thickness, and two more to 3/16″, then cut them in two and match them as pairs. The bottom edges are cut to match the curve of the stem, which is much more pronounced on the thinner leading pairs. They are also thinned slightly along the bottom third of their lengths and beveled to fit tightly against the side of the stem when they are bent into the canoe. I have had water heating with the few remaining half ribs soaking in it while I prepared the cant ribs, and now I place then in the pot as well. While they soften, I

The planking is at last fastened to the stems. Fastening is alternated from side to side to prevent the stem from twisting.

The cant ribs beveled for insertion into the ends of the hull.

This multi-faceted hollow clinching iron will fit nicely against any surface in the canoe's interior. GC

install the remaining half ribs, using the clinching iron to back up the driven tacks. Life would be tough around the canoe shop without this little device, which is of cast iron and designed with a number of surfaces to match the many contours found inside the canoe. It is hollow as well, reducing its weight, and making it easy to hold and turn. Lacking a proper clinching iron, you could accomplish the job using autobody dollies, and for limited repairwork, almost anything of solid metal which does not dent the cedar will suffice.

When I've finished with the half ribs, including the replacement of the split one, I inspect the ends of all those already in the canoe to see which need additional fastening. Not wishing to split any during the planking process, I stopped nailing them well before reaching the ends, and now I use ½″ tacks wherever necessary to make the ends conform to the hull. Still, I am careful not to place the tacks closer than ¾″ from the ends.

By the time this is done, the cant ribs are ready. I select one of the thicker ones and introduce a little bend into the thinned lower end before placing it in the canoe. Then I set the lower end in position, and push down on the top enough to finish bowing the bottom into the proper shape to conform to the planking without distorting it. If the beveled surface against the stem is not quite a perfect fit, I take the rib out and adjust the bevel with a finger plane. Once it fits, I check to ensure the spacing is correct relative to the last rib, top and bottom, then nail it in place holding the clinching iron on the inside. A thinner cant rib is placed ahead of the first, adjusted, and similarly fastened. Then I fish out the mates to these two and install them on the opposite side of the stem — struggling all the while, because I have never become adept at driving tacks left-handed.

Before fastening the cant ribs to the gunwales, I must first shape the tops so the outside gunwale will fit flush against them. The outwale will be running alongside at a very shallow angle to its joint with the inwale at the tip. I can get a good fit by tapering the top inch (about the depth of the gunwale) of the two cant ribs plus the last whole rib, from full thickness at the trailing edge to ¹⁄₁₆″ less at the leading edge. A canoe with a fuller bow might require somewhat sharper tapers. This time the wood to be removed comes off the inside surface of the ribs.

To accomplish this I mark the tapers on the tops of the ribs, then sliding my Japanese saw beneath the deck I score the ribs just below the gunwale, holding the saw at an angle that approximates the taper. I use a chisel to remove the tapered sliver from the top, and smooth up the cut with a

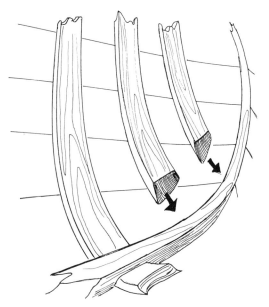

Installing the beveled and tapered cant ribs.

rasp. When I've treated all three on a side, I check the results by forcing them against the inwale with a piece of rib stock to approximate the outwale, and then make any adjustments required. Once I am satisfied, I nail the tapered ribs to the inwale with the bronze nails.

When I finish with both ends, I attack that split rib near the center of the canoe. I've learned through experience to spot and eliminate most ribs which, for one reason or another, will have a tendency to split during planking, but I surely missed this one and there are six or eight ugly longitudinal splits along it — and I know more will develop during the clinching process. Best just the take the whole thing out and replace it with a sound one. To ease the work of removing all those tacks, and minimize damage to the planking during the operation, I first work on the inside of the rib with an old screwdriver — digging it into the surface of the rib and straightening out the curled clinches or breaking them off. Then with the canoe turned upside down, I work my tack-puller gently under the heads and lift the shortened stubs out, meeting practically no resistance. I remove the bronze nails at the top, and tilting the bottom of the rib toward the center of the canoe I ease the whole thing out. Two wetted replacements (one of them a spare) are set in the steam box and the burner is already boiling the reduced amount of water I put in the milking pail for a quick steaming job.

While I wait, I start fitting the sheerstrake. It is a cut-and-fit proposition, with several angles to consider, but the job is made easier because everything can be marked from the inside now that the canoe is off the form. Here too, I try to avoid feather edges, and instead join my sections with beveled butt joints. The end of the sheerstrake is cut away enough to expose the inwale beyond the final cant rib; this will allow the outside gunwale to fit flush against it at the tip. It takes four sections plus a pair of small wedges to completely fill the space between the last course of planking and the top of the gunwale the whole length of the canoe, and I have saved some dark-colored, tight-grained stock to make it attractive. I won't have time to do the other side today, and the rib I am steaming is surely more than ready to be bent, so I turn my attention to that project.

I'll be using the canoe itself for a form since I've already raised the real form out of the way overhead with the blocks and tackle. I'll bend the new rib over the canoe one rib ahead of its actual position to make up for the difference in the tightness of the curve between the inside and outside of the hull. I slide the hot, wet rib out of the box and wrap it around the hull at the proper position. Then I clamp one end of it in place, half around to the other side of the

The sheerstrake is fitted and fastened once the decks and thwarts are installed.

Closeup of same. GC

The sheerstrake is cut back to expose final 6" of the inwale. GC

canoe, and rebend the rib more precisely, exactly as I would on the form — stretching it as much as possible before clamping it fast. I set a 12-pound box of tacks on the middle of it to hold that portion flat against the bottom of the canoe, and leave it to set overnight.

April 23

We heard our first spring peeper last evening by the pool below the ruined dam; a soloist, who as though suffering from stage fright, began very cautiously. I was barely conscious of his efforts when he stopped, testing the reaction of the audience before daring to proceed. I had almost dismissed the notion when he started again, a little longer this time and loud enough for a positive audio identification over the rush of water. There were a few more pauses and false starts, then he launched into a chorus that went uninterrupted for several minutes.

The marvel was that the tiny frog could sing at all last night. The sun went down dragging the chill wind behind it, but the sky was without a cloud and by the time the first stars poked through, when our little friend began singing, it was already getting very cold. I'd been raking up the winter rubble that each winter takes up residence in our yard, comfortable in a sweater and wool jacket. This thumbnail-sized creature, naked in his world of ice water and frigid mist should have been frozen solid — a silent inanimate ice object suggesting the life forms that will later thrive under the hot summer sun.

Still, he sang on for a bit, though not for long. It was a piece suited to a choir, and failing to muster any support, he despaired, surrendering to the over-whelming evidence that he was simply ahead of his time.

Unfinished Business

Town business takes up a chunk of time each week, and this morning I faced the music and drove into the shire-town on a variety of errands. For once everyone and everything were where I thought they'd be, and I was in my shop ready to start work at 10.

The first item of business is the rib wrapped around the hull ready for installation. When I unclamp it from the gunwales it straightens out considerably, but once in the canoe it will conform easily enough to its intended shape and I am glad to have a little resilience left in it for adjustments I'll need to make. I've marked the position of the gunwales on the rib so there is no guesswork regarding its exact situation in the canoe. The rib is slid into position sideways, the way its predecessor came out, and the ends are temporarily clamped to the gunwales. Then, working with one end, I bear down on the top slightly and bow the curved portion against the planking with my other hand until it fits snuggly without distorting either the side or bottom of the hull. I reclamp it, put in a few tacks to hold it in place then go around and fit the other side. When it is completely tacked in, I cut it off at the ends to match the others — and I'm finished.

I fit the sheer planks on the remaining side using the same pattern as on the first, then with the utility knife I cut down any high areas that extend above the gunwale. A small lip to cover the top of the planking and canvas will be rabbeted into the outside gunwale so that only the tops of the ribs will show between the two rails. To accommodate this shelf, the top of the sheer plank must be cut evenly $3/8''$ below the top surface of the inwales the length of the canoe. I use a wooden marking gauge that holds a pencil at the proper level to mark a line on the planking as the device is drawn along the gunwale. Once marked, the plank is neatly trimmed to the proper height by several passes with the utility knife.

The metal bands have done a fair job of clinching over many of the tacks on the inside of the canoe while it was being planked on the form. Many others, however, are not quite satisfactory and will need to be further set against the clinching iron. The clinched portions must be totally depressed into the wood of the interior; by the same token, the oval heads must be at or below the level of the outside of the planking before the hull can be finished. It is easier to simply go over the entire canoe, iron in one hand and hammer in the other, striking each of the tacks to ensure the proper set. This can be physically tiring as well as monotonous, but is absolutely essential. I am thankful that I have arms that indicate my early primate ancestry, because with one side of the canoe tilted up off the horses slightly, I can reach with the iron clear to the garboard seam and still see what my hammer is doing on the outside of the hull.

Tack by tack and rib by rib, I work my way down one side of the canoe developing a nice rhythm. The idea is to not crush the surrounding wood each time a tack is struck. I reaffirm that I am backing and striking the same tack by

first giving the head a light tap. If the clinching iron is in the proper place the strike will feel solid on both iron and hammer; otherwise the hammer will bounce off the planking, and I'll hear a hollow sound that tells me I need to adjust the position of the iron. The second rap is sounder, although still not brutal. It not only feels right, but normally there will be a little metallic ring indicating the tack has been properly seated. Each time a rib is completed I run my hand along on the inside. If I've done my job properly, it will not catch on or scratch across any protruding brass. The clinching iron is always held along the rib, never across it, and it should never be bridged across the turn of the bilge, because either situation will result in little grooves or lines depressed into the wood, and they are the devil to sand out. Rows of "hammer blossoms" develop along the rib lines on the outside of the hull, but these can be easily eliminated later, so long as the fibers aren't broken or badly crushed.

It takes me a good part of the afternoon to clinch the entire canoe. Later, before I leave for the night, I will liberally apply hot water to the rows of hammer marks and by morning 90 percent of them will have swollen flush with the surface of the hull, leaving the heads well depressed in the wood. Some of those that don't swell out will be eliminated during the sanding operation, and any dimples remaining will be tiny and spanned by the taut canvas skin.

This simple marking jig scribes a line along the sheerstrake for final trimming. GC

To make the clinching task a little more bearable, the canoe is tilted at a modest angle. GC

A short-based orbital sander fitted with a foam pad is the best tool for sanding the contours inside the hull. GC

I sand the interior of the ribs with a short-based orbital sander fitted with a foam pad on the base, using plenty of 120-grit paper. The sander is applied along the ribs in several passes and cleans up the stains, small dents, and fuzz that have accumulated during the building process. The cant ribs up under the deck are sanded by hand, first with 80-grit then 120-grit sandpaper. The edges of the ribs are hand-sanded with 120-grit paper, folded over. Here I am careful not to contact the perpendicular planking with the sandpaper and scratch it across the grain. By the end of the day I am rewarded by the clean, crisp look of the freshly sanded interior, the lovely unfinished white cedar pure and smooth with an almost satin texture. It is actually much prettier now to my eye than it will be with the varnish finish; but of course the soft, gleaming wood without the protective coating would soon weather a dull gray and be irretrieveably soiled with ground-in dirt and sand.

After applying hot water to the exterior of the hull to swell out the hammer marks, I shut off the power and lock up the shop for the night.

April 24

Last night after supper I paddled my canoe for the first time this season, on the stream running past the house. I poled down the rapid section, and around the S-turn into the deep, round pool. Below this point the stream is under the influence of the big beaver dam a mile downstream, although at this time of the year there is still plenty of current and it was an easy paddle, gliding along with the swiftly moving sheet of meltwater. There are many turns to build the anticipation, and along much of the route, alder-rimmed meadows, now flooded, extend out to the stream from the woods. There were black ducks sharing the stream with me, plus a pair of muskrats, and I was pleased to see a beaver between the lodge and the dam. I feared a trapper, whose underwater sets were marked by poles sticking through the ice last winter, would catch them all, and neglected, the great dam would gradually slip away with the current.

The paddle back was invigorating work, testing muscles that hadn't been properly flexed since freeze-up. Poling the final section, against the flood in near darkness, was the most satisfying. The old White rose to the challenge, recalling all the refinements of the route up the little rapids that made the passage safe and enjoyable.

Overnight, most of the hammer marks disappeared as I had anticipated, the soaked wood swelling out to its original configuration. Still, in order to get the hull smooth enough for canvasing, the outside of the planking must be faired and sanded smooth. The clinching succeeded in pulling the planking more tightly against the ribs, but there are still small ridges along the plank seams, which I can feel when I run my hand along the hull. These are most prevalent at the turn of the bilge and up in the quarters of the canoe. Planking lines distinguishable through the canvas detract from any canoe, and I find it beneficial to shave off these little ridges before I start sanding.

Most of the tack heads are buried safely out of the way, but I still exercise considerable caution as I slide my spokeshave along the raised seams. Luckily for me the fastenings are brass and not steel, because I manage to strike a few each time I do this. Because the brass is relatively soft, the edge of the blade is seldom badly nicked. When I've done my best with the edge tool, I press my fairing block back into service, using it just as I did initially on the backside of the ribs, pushing and pulling it across the curves of the hull, the block parallel to the planking. Ten minutes to a side with this device usually takes care of the fairing, although it also inadvertently leaves scratches, which for the most part will be sanded out.

There is a bright April sun warming the air outside and just enough breeze to carry away the fine airborn dust, so I move horses and canoe outside for the power-sanding operation. My strategy will be to finish fairing and sand out most of the scratches with the power disc sander, equipped with a foam feathering disc and 80-grit sandpaper. Then

Fairing and Canvasing

A disc sander is used to fair and smooth the hull's exterior. GC.

using 60-grit paper on a long-based orbital sander, I will accomplish the final smoothing.

Fairing with the disc sander can be tricky until you get the hang of it. The pad must be kept moving, and it must be held flat on the surface and tangent to the curves, or flat spots are sure to materialize. I get the feel of this noisy machine each time by first concentrating on the relatively flat bottom section, moving it along the surface with and then across the planking. With my confidence building, I work on the ends, which are also large surfaces with gentle curves, but sit in a vertical rather than horizontal plane. This gives me the feel of the machine working smoothly up and down perpendicular to the planking. Finally I do the bilge area and the sides, working the disc quickly back and forth across the curve while at the same time slowly advancing it along the hull.

It is tempting to stop here, and the hull looks and feels very smooth after the disc sander has done its work, but the surface can still be improved by some work with the orbital sander.

The base of this machine has a thin felt pad as a cushion for the 60-grit paper, and it too is applied mainly across the hull, the machine itself parallel to the planking lines. Because I don't have to move as fast with this sander — it cuts much more slowly than the disc unit — I can concentrate on smoothing out spots left just a little lumpy by the disc sander. I stop once the hull is as fair and smooth as I can get it with the 60-grit paper. Continuing with a finer-grit abrasive at this point will only polish the hull, and I am more interested in leaving a little texture in the wood. The shop vacuum cleaner rids the surface and the seams of the fine, clinging dust.

It's a good idea to treat the outside of the hull with some sort of oil that will minimize the cedar's tendency to soak up the water that gets sloshed into the canoe. I like boiled linseed oil because it "waxes over" as it dries, providing a good seal. It is also fully compatible with my canvas filler; so should I choose, I can apply it to the hull the same day I plan to canvas and fill. To the oil I add about 20 percent clear Cuprinol wood preservative to increase its penetrating ability as well as to discourage the growth of mildew beneath the canvas. Usually I heat the solution somewhat short of the boiling point before application, which also reduces the mixture's viscosity. Just before lunch, I lay on a heavy coat of this oil mixture, using about a quart, and leave the canoe out in the sun and wind to dry. When I return, everything will be ready for stretching the canvas.

Cotton canvas comes in a variety of grades and weights, and it is manufactured by factories throughout the world. I always specify Grade A Domestic Midwest Duck, which is woven to rigid specifications for the tightness of the weave and shrinkage factors. I am assured by representatives of the industry that the same standards are observed by the mills operated in Brazil by American companies, but that much of the imported canvas from the Near and Far East is inferior in quality and subject to considerable shrinkage.

"Numbered" duck is purportedly superior to "ounce" duck, which is labeled according to its actual weight in ounces per square yard. The labeling system on the Midwest duck I use does not correspond directly to its actual weight, and in fact the higher numbers designate the lighter fabrics. Number 10, which is the weight I generally prefer, actually weighs 13 or 14 ounces per yard. Number 8 duck is the most common weight found in canoe building and is certainly thicker and stronger than Number 10, but it is also a good deal heavier — heavier, I feel, than most canoeists require, and all but the more avid whitewater enthusiasts would be better served by the lighter weight. Not only will the lighter raw canvas weigh less, but it will require less of the heavy filler to finish it, and it will soak up less water later on. On smaller canoes designed for solo paddling, or for packing into remote ponds for fishing and hunting, I would recommend the very light Number 12 canvas which is considerably lighter still. You will have to be your own judge of what weight canvas will best serve your needs. Today, on this general-purpose 18-footer, I will be using the Number 10.

Canvasing a hull using a single folded piece of dry cotton duck is an interesting project, one that was perfected long ago by canoe manufacturers to the point that one can scarcely improve upon their results and efficiency. The shape of the canoe is very complex, when you consider it must be completely wrapped in a sheet of fabric so that the skin is uniformly taut and fits perfectly without the introduction of darts or gores. Fortunately, canvas stretches nicely, and by balancing out the tension applied to the canvas horizontally with that applied laterally around the hull, this seemingly impossible task becomes a simple routine matter.

My outfit is modeled after those used by the large canoe companies and consists of a boat-trailer winch bolted to a post at one end of the shop and a bent iron strap bolted to the opposing wall as an anchoring point. Two 4' hardwood clamps hinged at the top, with interlocking tongue-and-groove jaws, clamp the canvas tightly at each end. The beam above provides a solid overhead for bracing the canoe down into the suspended canvas and is also an anchoring point from which the maple clamps are hung.

These hardwood clamps trap the canvas envelope and allow it to be stretched by a winch or come-along.

Rollin stretching the canvas taut. GC

The tension is slightly reduced and the hull placed in the envelope.

After wiping off any excess oil from the hull, I roll out about seven yards of canvas on top of it, enough so I have at least a foot to work with beyond the canoe at each end, and carefully fold it in half lengthwise. This is the envelope into which the canoe will be placed for the actual canvasing process. I slide the suspended clamp at one end of the shop along a pipe to adjust the distance between the two clamps, keeping them slightly farther apart than the length of the canoe. Then, with the open end up, I close the folded canvas into the clamps and tighten down the bolts that lock them closed. I secure one end to the wall using a chain, then hook the winch cable to the opposite end. Slowly, I take up the slack, with the winch stretching the envelope until it is taut. I figure it is tight enough when I can tap it with my finger and produce a muffled drumming sound, and I mark the cable with a piece of tape at the winch drum

as a reference. I must relieve most of the tension in order to place the canoe into the fold, and I'll need to know how much tension to reintroduce once the canoe is in place. Both ends are nestled down into the canvas as deeply as possible, and I make sure the stems are aligned with the clamps, and that there are equal amounts of excess above the gunwales on both sides. Satisfied of this, I crank the winch until the cable is within an inch or two of its former position. As the winch pulls the canvas, the envelope is compressed, raising the canoe considerably inside its hammock and actually threatening to expel the hull should I continue tightening. Now I must match this horizontal tension with pressure applied vertically to push the canoe back down into the sling and force the canvas to form around the hull. To neutralize the considerable tension, I must introduce a great deal of weight into the canoe.

The easiest and most effective way to do this, although it may look dramatic to the uninitiated, is to climb aboard the suspended hull and walk up and down the length of it. The bottom is protected by a padded board which distributes my weight and prevents me from putting my foot through the hull. Near the ends, I rock back and forth to settle the hull as deeply as possible into the hammock. Such an exercise improves your balance if you're a poler, but if the idea doesn't appeal to you, you can achieve the same end by loading down the canoe, especially in the

The canoe braced down into its canvas fold.

Using a come-along to stretch the canvas. GC

quarters, with bags of sand or cement or anything comparable. With my method, the canoe is braced down from the ceiling beam in each quarter with sections of 2x2, and I even have a pair of steps (fashioned from progressively longer bits of 2x6s) which I use as a variable base to increase or decrease the pressure.

When the proper balance is reached, the canvas will conform to the hull along the bottom and sides with just a little crease or fold along the flat run of the stems. The excess canvas above the sheerline tends to fold itself in over the canoe like little taut canvas decks. There are normally a few wrinkles extending from where the canvas "breaks" from the curve of the stem, running at a slight upwards angle to the hardwood clamp. Too many wrinkles here, especially if the canoe has forced the canvas way below the bottom of the clamps and they run up at a steep angle, indicate excessive vertical pressure. Of course, I

Canvasing set up.

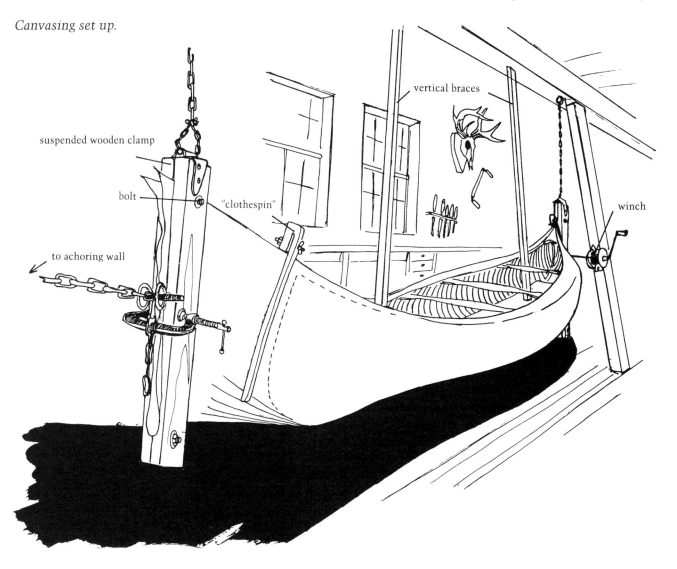

suspended wooden clamp

bolt

"clothespin"

to achoring wall

vertical braces

winch

can't check all of these things without climbing out of the canoe, and frequently I must step aboard more than once before everything is satisfactory. Today the only adjustment required is a couple more turns on the winch handle.

The excess canvas is cut a couple inches above the sheer the length of the canoe on both sides, and a long clothespin-type clamp made from a length of ash board brings the two edges of the material together just beyond the ends of the decks.

To pull the canvas taut at each rib for fastening, I use a pair of artist's canvas-stretching pliers — equipped with elongated jaws grooved on the inside to provide a firm grip. Upholsterer's pliers or those nasty clawed devices that initially rip the fabric before catching hold can also be effective. Scraps of rib stock cushion the gunwale from the butt of the grips, which are centered at each rib for pulling. It's important not to pull the canvas too hard at this point or little scallops develop between the ribs where the fabric relaxes; these are very noticeable when glossy finish paint is applied. Once I have a good grip, I simply rock the pliers inboard about 45 degrees, then drive two tacks 1/8" below the top edge of the planking, centered on the rib, about 3/4" apart. When the pliers release their grip, a tiny fold of canvas is formed directely over the fastenings. I begin pulling and nailing amidships and work up one side all the way to the deck. It is a waste of time at this point to fasten

The canvas at the end of the canoe before it is slit to form an overlapping seam.

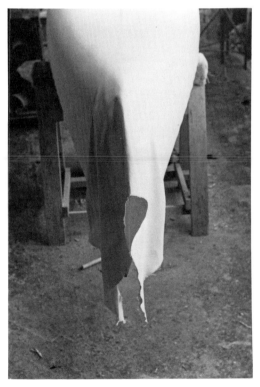

Along the gunwale the canvas is gripped at each rib end by artist's pliers, and the pliers rocked inboard about 45 degrees.

the canvas beyond the final full rib. Instead, I return to the middle of the canoe and work along in the opposite direction on the same side. The little creases in the canvas under the stems have disappeared, as I expected, and I go around the canoe to begin fastening the canvas along the remaining side.

Before removing the vertical braces and cutting the canoe free, I check to ensure I haven't accidentally trapped something irretrievable between the canvas and the hull. The canvas is cut beyond the long clothespins, which prevents me from cutting the canvas too close to the stem to make the required overlapping seam, and I put the canoe upside down on horses where I can best do up the ends.

The canvas is tight all along the canoe up to the fastening at the last full rib. Beyond this point, it droops past and over the stem in a loose fold. I must locate the point on the stem where this rib passes through the notch and slit the canvas from that point straight out to the very end, converting the single fold into two separate flaps which will form the overlapping seam. A light layer of bedding compound is smeared along the stem before I start.

First, I grip both flaps a few inches beyond the start of the slit and pulling them slightly ahead, cross them one over another for a couple of inches to start the overlapping process. I drive several $1/4''$ copper tacks through both layers and into the stem to secure them, then fold the upper layer out of the way and concentrate on the inner layer. To make the pulling more effective, I first grab the canvas just beyond the ends of the gunwales and pull it very hard forward, along the run of the gunwales toward the end. This reduces the size of the fold that developed forward of the last canvas fastener when the tension was released. One of the larger tacks driven into the gunwale at about the junction with the stem prevents the canvas from relaxing once I let go. With the flap secured at its origin at the turn of the stem and also at the gunwale, I now concentrate on pulling the flap around the stem and fastening it about every $1/2''$ with the $1/4''$ copper tacks. The canvas is pulled perpendicular to the curve of the stem as I progress towards the gunwales working with 3" sections of the canvas. The tacks are placed just to the far side of an imaginary centerline running down the stem. Once fastened, the excess canvas is trimmed just outside the row of tacks, and another layer of bedding compound is applied before the second lap is brought over and fastened. The tacks are driven between those of the under layer in the same line, so when the canvas is carefully trimmed the raw edge will run very nearly down the stem's centerline where it is most effectively covered by the brass stemband. To complete the end,

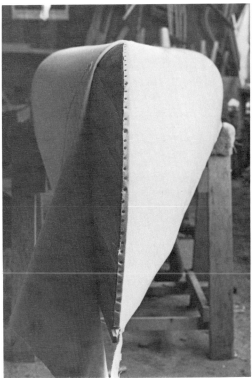

The canvas is pulled "normal off" around the curves of the stem for fastening.

One side fastened and trimmed.

The completed seam.

Cutting the second lap.

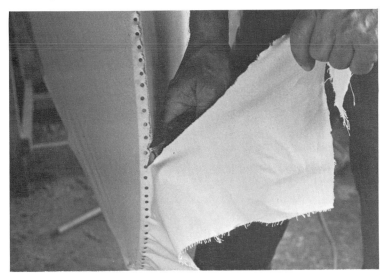

Scorching the cotton nap with a torch.

I pull and fasten the canvas at the sheer at each end of the cant ribs. To eliminate the fold behind the tack on the last full rib, I release the canvas here, repull it with the pliers, and refasten. The fold reappears behind the next tack down the line but is greatly reduced in size. When both ends are completed, I break out the propane torch and scorch the entire canvas surface by holding the nozzle at a very shallow angle to the surface and slowly moving the torch across the hull in 2" swaths. The deflected flame burns off the nap and fuzz that make it difficult to get a smooth filling job. So long as I keep the torch moving, there is little danger of igniting the canoe. I am especially careful not to catch on fire any of the loose threads at the edges. These act like little fuses, burning up to the canvas itself where, if left alone, they would burn a little furrow a couple of threads wide that would essentially cut the canvas in two.

My final step before quitting for the night is applying Cuprinol to the canvas along the sheer and stem seams — a measure to discourage mildew from growing and rotting the edge of the canvas beneath the outwale.

April 25

On my walk to work, I pass a pasture where some Herefords stoically outlasted the winter, well fed, but with only the surrounding woods for shelter. On bright, sunny mornings like today's they bask in the warmth, stretching their shaggy chestnut and white forms across the brown grass of the east-facing hillside, soaking up the sun's rays. They are finally expelling the last of the winter's cold, which during the siege had clenched its frigid fingers around their very cores.

Soon little white heads will dot the field alongside the larger ones as the first calves arrive. Then the quiet pastoral scene will become animated. The ebullient youngsters, too curious to waste the golden days comatose, bounce and romp among the patient, wiser, cud-chewing survivors.

Filling the Weave

The canvas filler is designed to fill the weave, providing a smooth surface for the exterior finish while it also waterproofs. Most fillers won't penetrate the canvas 100 percent, but nonetheless they greatly reduce the amount of water the canvas can absorb. Most of today's fillers are oil-based, and although good, are not as effective as the old white lead-based fillers which appear to have enjoyed a longer life. Unfortunatley, the men who worked with the lead compounds may not have shared this longevity, at least not without some ill effects to their health. The soft lead kept the filler flexible indefinitely, and additionally, mildew could not thrive on canvas saturated with this toxic element and this prevented the canvas from rotting around the edges.

The linseed oil-based fillers secretly concocted by canoe manufacturers in the '50s use a thickening agent — normally, finely powdered silica or quarz (Silex) — which allows the substance to cure to a hard slate-like finish over a period of two to six weeks. Many small canoe shops still use them.

Some of today's builders are enjoying satisfactory results using latex paint-based systems which are built up on the outside of the canvas to a smooth surface which is very flexible initially. The stuff is very tough, I am advised, but since none of the canvas is actually filled, I worry that the canvas will absorb too much water later, adding to the canoe's weight on a trip and increasing the amount of shrinkage.

Foul-smelling airplane dopes that set up quickly are preferred by still others, who use the compound primarily to cut down on weight. In the hands of professionals, skilled in working with airplane fabrics, the resulting finish can be very good, although a bit more textured than that of the conventional fillers. I have seen some amateur efforts using this dope, however, and they have not been so great. My experience has been almost exclusively with the the oil-based fillers and results have been satisfactory, although I am sometimes tempted to experiment with the white lead mixtures — exercising what precautions I can to minimize the health hazards.

Canvasing a Square Stern

If you choose to canvas a square-sterned canoe or boat by the winch-and-clamp method, you will need an extra 5-6' of canvas at the transom end, instead of the usual foot or so of excess with a double-ender. Otherwise, the canvas will not properly form around the contours of the transom and be stretched uniformly around the perimeter. It is also important to tack the canvas along the gunwale all the way to the end while the canoe is still in the sling under tension.

There have been several methods developed to attach the canavas at the transom, but one of the simplest and most effective with boats that have transoms rabbeted for the ends of the planking proceeds as follows:

Once the boat is cut free, the protruding canvas at the stern is nearly trimmed to within ½" all the way round. This excess is neatly tucked beneath itself exactly at the edge, so there are no exposed frayed edges. A bead of caulking or bedding compound is worked under the doubled edge with a putty knife. Then, starting at the keel line and working around to the gunwales, the canvas is fastened to the transom's edge with small copper wire nails or ¼" tacks spaced every ¼".

Another method commonly used has the excess canvas — trimmed to about an inch from the transom — simply folded around the corner of the stern, bedded, and tacked. The fold of canvas around the transom is then covered by fitted trim pieces bedded and screwed to the transom.

Filling is a big job when you're doing a large canoe alone as I am today. I first apply a liberal coat, using a wide brush which has the bristles cut down to about 1-½" in length, spreading the filler on 3' section on one side of the hull and working it into the weave with a tight circular motion of the brush. The filler dries almost instantly and is followed by a liberal second coat, which is slathered on thickly and evenly. In a couple minutes the wet coat begins to dull or fade, indicating it too is drying, and I begin rubbing it vigorously, using a thumbless mitt made from canvas scraps, back and forth across the section and in a circular pattern as well. It's important to work this coat deeply into the fabric in order to fill as much of the canvas as possible. Light rubbing here will eventually smooth the filler but will not make it penetrate the canvas as deeply as it should.

The surface is soon dry and smooth and I concentrate on redistributing the filler with the mitt, treating a few small patches where the weave of the fabric is still evident, usually on the sides, which always seem a little more difficult to fill than the bottom. If the surface of the filled canvas is uniformly smooth with a soft satin finish, this second coat may be enough. Generally, however, I apply a very light third coat, cut with mineral spirits about 10 percent. This coat is likewise rubbed with the mitt, but not as hard. My goal this time is to distribute the filler as evenly as possible on the existing surface, and I rub for a long time before the surface is dry and as smooth as I like. Near the end I remove the mitt and work the nearly dry section with the palms of my hands. When it is perfectly smooth, with just the hint of a light peach fuzz on the surface, I have finished and can begin another section. The seams at the stems are treated with a buildup of many coats of filler rubbed thoroughly until there is no trace of the raw edges.

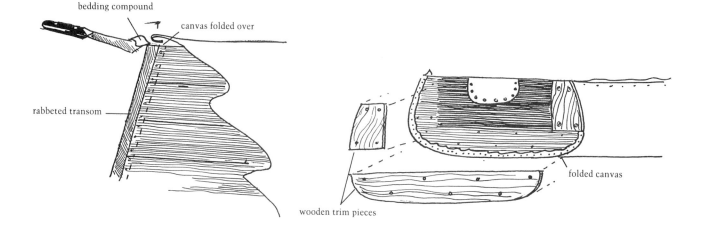

bedding compound

canvas folded over

rabbeted transom

folded canvas

wooden trim pieces

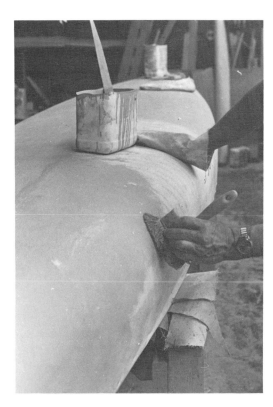

Rubbing the second coat smooth with a canvas mitt. A third coat is usually required.

Applying the initial coat of filler with a brush with shortened bristles.

The completed filling job should result in a satin-smooth hull.

I take my time working the length of the canoe. It is easy to fatigue the arm and pectoral muscles necessary for proper rubbing, and the subsequent finish would suffer. It's monotonous work, although not unpleasant like the application of fiberglass or epoxy. It is a reflective time when my mind has the freedom to wander where it will as I move steadily along, the spring sunlight bathing the shop.

I am pleased with the progress and results so far. The smooth, gray bottom of the canoe suggests the back of a dolphin or whale. I've put flesh and hide on the skeleton that was sitting on the form a week ago, and soon I'll have to put it aside for a time while the filler seasons. Eventually it will be equipped to begin its new life, serving a master who I hope will be kind and caring, but who will not deny the canoe the opportunity to taste under competent guidance the wide variety of elements for which it was designed and built.

May 25

The salmon I nearly landed last evening was not especially large, but like all of her kind was graced with a spirit that refused domination. In the beginning, strength and stamina were almost enough to carry the contest for her. Her split-second responses and magnificent vaults kept me constantly off balance, and it was I who was reacting to her initiatives. Still, the leader was sound, and I was patient enough not to force things; so with the streamer lodged firmly in the corner of her mouth, the cards were stacked against her. Denied the opportunity to rest, she would soon succumb to exhaustion and the net — or so I thought.

But at the last instant, when she appeared completely spent, fanning her tailfin feebly alongside the canoe as the net dipped in her direction, some hidden reserve was tapped. The response released by this immediate threat was explosive, and the convulsive roll brushed her past the rim of the net which snagged the fly, tearing it from the tough skin. Dazed, she paused briefly, then slowly sounded into the depths of the pool, leaving behind a surprised angler swelling with admiration for her and all her kind.

Paint and Varnish — and Gunwales, Seats, and Stembands

Next week the owner will be by to pick up his new canoe. We'll load it atop his car and it will be off to New York State. In July it will travel to the Boundary Waters Canoe Area of Minnesota and the adjacent Quetico, where it will carry its owner through that delightful tangle of lakes and water courses, and in turn, be carried by him over the numerous portages.

I'm satisfied with the fourth coat of the royal blue paint that was applied yesterday, and it won't need a fifth as I had feared. The masking tape is pulled from the gunwales, and now they will require a fourth and final coat of varnish after a light sanding. I must also install the stembands and the caned seats. An ⅛"-wide pin-stripe tape like that used on automobiles will define the waterline between the orange shellac bottom and the blue topsides, and I can finish all of this today.

A little over a week ago, I lowered the canvased hull from

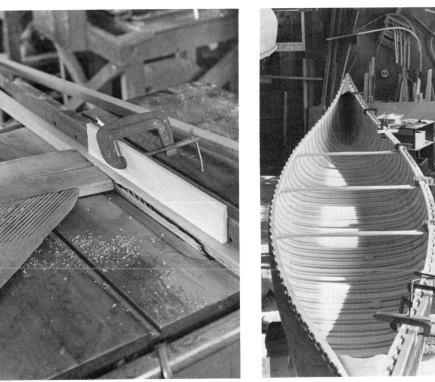

Cutting the outwale rabbet on the table saw; note the use of featherboards. GC

The outwale is clamped along the sheer for fastening.

its perch below the 16′ form where it had been drying since it was filled. When I tried to dig out a chunk with my thumbnail, it simply scratched across the surface. I install the gunwales before painting the canoe, because otherwise the tender paint gets nicked and scratched during the rail installation and varnishing process. I also like to seal the seam between the inside edge of the gunwale and the canvas with the paint to prevent water running down inside.

The full-length mahogany gunwale stock measures $^{15}/_{16}$″ deep by $^{3}/_{4}$″ wide before rabbeting. There were a number of blanks already sawn and planed to these dimensions, so I selected a pair, clamped them to the the bench, and pre-sanded the tops, bottoms, and outsides with the belt sander. The lip that covers the top of the planking and canvas is $^{3}/_{16}$″ wide and $^{1}/_{4}$″ deep. The wood is removed by a dado set up on the table saw. I first set the blades to the proper height and distance from the fence and run a scrap piece through to check the setup. After any minor adjustments, I run about 2′ of the actual stock through, then stop the saw and set up featherboards. Accuracy is important here, and whenever dealing with long, awkward lengths, such a precaution makes sense. The featherboards hold the gunwales flush against table and fence, and all I do is push the stock through, then clean up the cut here and there with the chisel. Had the inwale been beveled as on a canoe with tumblehome, this cut would have been made at a complementary angle.

The excess canvas is cut carefully along the top edge of the sheer plank, the knife angled slightly down to prevent any canvas from protruding above the planking. I start clamping the outwale onto the canoe amidships and use as many C-clamps as necessary to hold it securely in place. Since I'll be fastening the rail at every second rib, I keep this in mind when placing the clamps and I use scrap pieces of planking to protect the gunwales inside and out.

The relative heights of the gunwales are constantly checked and kept even. When necessary, I use a section of stock placed across both gunwales and clamped below the inwale to force the outwale down into the proper plane. On models that have tight curves near the ends, the outwales are pre-bent on a jig just as the inwales were. I stop clamping a yard from the end, bring the gunwale up along the inwale, and cut it to length. The lip must be removed at a gradual angle at the end to allow the outwale to sit flush against the inwale. Marking a neat taper about 5" long, I shave the wood away with a block plane. The remainder of the gunwale can then be clamped in place and the same procedure followed to attach the other end. I drill the holes for the 1-½" No. 8 bronze screws at every other rib, countersinking the flat heads so they are barely below the surface. Care is taken with the electric screwdriver, guarding against slippage which could ruin the slot of a screw or even the wood around it. I put a screw in each of the last three ribs to pull the gunwale in flush against the tapered tops.

The belt sander with a fresh 80-grit belt is used to sand the tops of the ribs flush with the gunwales. It is applied in slow, steady passes the whole length of the canoe until the ribs are cut down flush. A back-and-forth motion across the rib tops would cause the sander to rock and dig into the gunwale between ribs, resulting in valleys and scallops that show up when the rails are finished. The belt sander is also used to neatly round and polish the top ends of the jointed gunwales. The top edges of the gunwales inside and out are very slightly relieved using the spokeshave, then I spend a couple hours hand-sanding the rails using a sanding block and 80-grit then 120-grit sandpaper, until it looks ready to finish. The addition of the dark mahogany outwales and the neat appearance of the two gunwales with the polished ends of the ribs spaced evenly between have added a great deal to the beauty of the canoe, and it is easy at this point to envision the finished product.

Because of the porous nature of white cedar, a sealing agent may be recommended by the manufacturer before applying the varnish. Some products require only that the first coat be cut with a small percentage of thinner. Although there have been big improvments in some of the clear polyurethane finishes in recent years, the traditional spar varnish with a slight orange tint is the most appropriate for this type of canoe and affords the longest protection to the wood both against the weathering action of sun and moisture and the physical abuses wrought upon the canoe during use.

Like everyone else, I like the idea of an oil finish and appreciate the smooth satin look of a hull freshly treated with tung oil or one of the other oil products. However, in the long run — and even relatively short run — such products do not supply the ideal protection for this soft, porous wood. The oil systems that eventually build up to a hard finish require far too many coats to be practical in a canoe. The cedar drinks up coat after coat gaining weight with each one, with no indication that the finish will actually build up to a protective layer. Such products work best on close-grained, dense hardwoods. The ordinary oil finishes soon darken considerably, and dirt that is easily hosed or scrubbed off a varnish finish is not so easily

The rails and rib tops are hand-sanded smooth after belt sanding.

The thwarts may be temporarily removed to facilitate varnishing the interior.

removed and ends up being ground into the surface of the wood.

I use a 2-½"-wide natural-bristle brush to apply the spar varnish in even strokes across the hull, one rib or space at a time. I had just enough time after sanding the outwales to lay down the first diluted coat. The following afternoon, I went over the interior with 220-grit sandpaper, taking care to get between the ribs and the edges of the ribs and half ribs as well. After a thorough vacuuming and cleaning with a tack rag, the interior was ready for the second coat, followed the next day by a third, again after a sanding with 220-grit then 400-grit paper. Occasionally, the whole canoe will need a fourth coat for an even gloss, but usually I reserve that for just the thwarts and gunwales.

Guides in Maine and New Brunswick, who frequently had to push their canoes over shallow gravel bars and negotiate summertime riffles, developed a system of finishing the exterior of the hull that made it stand up better to such abuse and easier to maintain on a regular basis. The unlikely agent that was applied to the canoe's bottom was a shellac, not the clear variety that turns white when exposed to moisture, but rather the pigmented orange shellac. It was their observation that the shellac formed a tougher surface than enamel paint, resisting scratching and peeling, and also made the bottom slipperier. The shellac had a tendency to dent rather than scratch when routine obstacles were encountered, and then swell back out later. Best of all, because of the alcohol base, most of the shellac simply oxidized away during the season, making it very easy to sand the bottom down whenever necessary and add fresh coats without the buildup problem caused by paint under such conditions. It didn't bother them that the shellac soon became crazed with hundreds of tiny cracks, because it was so fluid that these were filled each time a new coat was applied and they never caused any problems. For best results the shellac was applied directly over the filler, never over a coat of paint. The topsides of the canoe received much less abuse, and were painted in the conventional manner.

The system was a practical one for the professional guides, and it's valid today for someone who plans to do his canoeing under similar conditions. But since constant, shallow, fast-water work is the exception rather than the rule for most paddlers nowadays, it is not especially appropriate for everyone. Today's wooden canoe owners who use their canoes exclusively or primarily on flatwater would be better served by a proper marine enamel paint over the whole exterior of the canoe, including the bottom.

A few minor scratches accumulated over the season can be quite easily filled and painted over, eliminating the necessity of doing the whole bottom over each year, a requirement with the short-lived shellac.

This canoe is going to be one of today's exceptions — its owner is a fellow who does large amounts of wilderness traveling throughout the East and Canada, encountering a lot of quickwater during the season. He anticipates spending less time renewing the shellac each year than he now spends redoing the paint on his current canoe. The more meticulous guides would mark a waterline on the hull (usually allowing 6″ of freeboard above it amidships) to separate the shellacked bottom from the painted topsides. This resulted in an attractive two-tone pattern, and the waterline told the guide at a glance exactly how the canoe was trimmed. I learned this method of finishing a canoe from Garrett and Alexandra Conover, a pair of guides and wilderness travelers in the traditional manner, who in turn learned it from the late Francis E. Fahey, noted Maine guide, boatbuilder, and teacher of Northwoods skills to the younger generations.

To get a perfect waterline, I set the canoe upside down on horses on the best section of the shop floor, leveling the canoe fore and aft as well as athwartships. I then determine an arbitrary waterline, normally 6″ from the sheerline at the center of the canoe. An adjustable three-legged stand that normally holds up one end of a roller used with the table saw is used to determine this height above the floor, and I fit the crosspiece at the top with a dowel equipped with a blunt nail for marking. Once the height is set, I can move the stand along the hull making as many as a dozen marks along the canoe. I fair the marks one to another by running a string around the hull from point to point, taping it lightly in place; any points that are out of line show up glaringly on the string, and I make the appropriate adjustments. Once established I add another dozen marks, using the string as a reference. It is then an easy matter to connect the marks with the masking tape. The filler is sanded by hand with 100-grit paper before any finish can be applied, and, of course, this is done before marking and taping the waterline.

Three-pound orange shellac dries very quickly, and I can apply all three coats in a single day. An hour after a coat is applied, it is ready for a light sanding with 400-grit paper and then the next coat. It must, however, dry overnight before masking tape can be affixed to it in order to begin painting the topsides. The outsides of the gunwales must also be masked for the painting job, but their bottom surfaces will be painted. Paint is far easier to maintain than varnish here, and it seals the seam where the gunwale meets the canvas.

Because I don't have a separate paint room in the shop, dust is a big problem for me when applying any finish. I try to schedule milling and sanding operations at times when I won't be finishing, but the fine dust which has saturated every corner and crevice of the shop over the years is always present. Fortunately, from early May on, I can run the exhaust fan for a few minutes before preparing for any finishing step, ridding the air of the fine particles.

Marine enamel paints that are most compatible with my filler are the most basic ones, and I stay away from those with an epoxy or acryllic base. Most of the paints I use are quite soft when first applied and remain that way for several weeks before reaching their optimum hardness. This makes them less durable than automobile or deck paint, but once cured, they are hard enough for good protection and over the long term stay more flexible, minimizing cracking and checking years later. In order to get the best possible finish when applying these paints with a brush, it is important to use the appropriate bushing liquids recommended by the manufacturer. These agents allow the paint to flow out smoothly as it dries, to a large extent eliminating the brush marks.

This is not the case with most of the recommended undercoaters, designed to prepare the surface for the final painting. These work well on wood surfaces, but are unpredictable on canvas. I used to use a coat or two of surfacing paint before the application of the finish, because even though the sanded filler feels perfectly smooth, there are little dips and hollows that the first coat or two of glossy finish paint will highlight. The undercoaters fill these imperfections nicely, and after sanding it was relatively easy to get a showroom finish with just two or three coats of paint. Later, however, bubbles or blisters would appear in the finish coat, although the undercoater would still be perfectly adhered to the filler. It didn't happen frequently, but it didn't take many times to scare me away from the practice. It may take more coats to achieve the same results using just the finish enamel, but it may well mean fewer problems down the line. My rule now is to apply all finishes directly to the filler. Since observing this simple principle, I've had no problems with paint adhesion.

I've been putting a coat of enamel on this canoe each of the past four days. As usual, the results of the first coat were disappointing. The surface I had considered smooth was pocked with little imperfections in the filler and the fluid paint, reduced even further by the brushing liquid, sought out and accented them all. This is always disheartening, but not unexpected. When it had dried the next day, I sanded it smooth with 180-grit then 220-grit wet-or-dry paper. Used with water, this abraisive cuts well and doesn't clog up with paint residue the way ordinary sandpaper does. The sanding removed all the paint from the high areas, leaving it in the low spots and depressions. The end product was an ugly, mottled appearance. The second coat of paint, reduced by an even greater amount of brushing fluid, looked much better than the first, although still left plenty of room for improvement. The sanding this time with the same grit wet-or-dry was not quite as thorough and the areas of paint left were much larger, as the surface began to even out. Sensing victory, I went over the entire canoe again, this time ending with 400-grit wet-or-dry. The third coat went on beautifully, and I felt certain I had succeeded in getting the finish I was seeking. An examination the next morning proved me wrong. As it dried, the paint shrank, receding into the tiniest little dimples and resulting in less than the first-class results I had counted on. How many more times it would surprise me like this I wasn't sure, but those were not cheerful thoughts that kept crossing my mind as I resanded the hull with the 400-grit paper.

That was yesterday, and as I brushed on the fourth coat, it looked just as good as the one before had. Luckily, this time the finish held and even improved as it dried, and today I can concern myself with the other finishing details.

I had made up seat frames earlier in the spring, planing down some ash to ⁷⁄₈″ and sawing it into strips 1-³⁄₈″ wide. The seat itself, measured to the inside of the frame, is 7-¹⁄₄x11″ but of course the crosspieces that extend to the gunwales are much longer than that, especially on the bow seats. When I make up a batch, I make them extra long and fit them each time to the individual canoe. I prefer a mortise-and-tenon joint to the dowelled variety, but either is acceptable. Including the ¹⁄₂″ tenons on each end, the short fore-and-aft sections of the seat frame are 8-¹⁄₄″ long. The tenons are cut on the radial arm saw, and the corresponding mortises cut by drilling two ³⁄₈″ holes side by side and cleaning the center with a chisel. I round the ends of the tenons to match the curved ends of the mortises, then clamp the frames together with bar clamps after carefully applying a waterproof glue that is made up from a powder. The next day I remove the frames from the clamps and give them a thorough sanding.

Natural cane is available in individual strands for hand-weaving, or in pre-woven sheets. The pre-woven sheets come in a variety of weaves from superfine with very small

The stern seat is normally placed up beneath the inwales and leveled with dowel spacers. GC

The mounting of the bow seat using dowels for spacers. GC

Details such as this mast step and supporting thwart deserve the builder's careful attention.

spaces and fine cane, to heavy with the opposite characteristics. The regular fine weave seems to be the most satisfactory. To prepare the frames for the sheets, a groove must be routered around the seat, centered on the frame members. A straight bit is used (carbide is almost a requirement) with a simple frame-type jig large enough to accommodate the base of the router, keeping the bit centered on the frame. The caned sheets are soaked in warm water and driven into the grooves with wooden wedges. For best results, I do one long side and then the opposite, then the two short sides in sequence. Excess cane is cut off with a chisel inside the groove, and a waterproof glue squeezed into the slots. The cane is held in place by sections of reed spline, cut to the proper lengths with mitered ends. These are also soaked in warm water and are tapped in place by a piece of wood, care being exercised not to crush the spongy material.

The caning for this canoe was hand-woven with individual strands (not by me, but by the neighbor up the road). After sanding the frames, all I needed to do was drill a series of $3/16''$ holes spaced $3/8''$ apart along each of the seat's four sides. To keep the wood from chafing and cutting the tight cane fibers, I eased the edges of the holes with a countersink both top and bottom. The caning process itself is time consuming and tough on soft fingers, but it is not difficult to learn, and instructions are provided by the companies that sell the supplies. It is a handy trick to know, not just for canoe work but for all those derelict rocking chairs moldering in the attic.

The stern seat is positioned nearer the end of the canoe than its counterpart in the bow, and is normally bolted right up against the gunwale. This combination gives the sternperson who must steer the canoe better control and improved visibility. It also raises the center of gravity, however, and it is up to the canoeist to learn when to abandon the seat in favor of kneeling a little forward when rough conditions are encountered. The bow seat is slung a little lower in the canoe, usually about 10" or 11" above the bottom. Like the stern seat, it it intended for comfort in flatwater situations and in rough water should be used only to lean against while kneeling on the bottom. I position the bow seat at the second and fourth ribs ahead of the quarter thwarts in the 18' canoe, and the stern seat on the sixth and seventh full rib from the end.

The frames are centered in place across the gunwales, perpendicular to the centerline of the canoe. Then I mark the crosspieces to the proper length and cut them on the bandsaw. Dowels are used as spacers to hold the seats at their respective levels, and these, after being cut to length,

A metal countersink bit can bore and countersink screw holes in the brass stemband in one easy operation.

The hollow contact surface of the keel is filled with bedding compound.

are pre-drilled with a ¼" bit. The seat must be level fore and aft and since there is a noticeable rise to the sheeerline over the space of three ribs, the forward dowels on the bow seat are longer than the aft ones — 1-3/8" and 7/8" respectively. The seat and dowels are carefully clamped into position and the 3/16" holes drilled through gunwale, dowel, and seat frame with a long bit. The stern seat frame is cut to length, and the forward crosspiece is notched to fit snugly against the gunwales. Dowels ¾" long are placed between the seat and gunwale aft to keep the seat level, and these are drilled and fastened. The little thwarts are also installed at this time by centering them in their positions just behind the decks. They come in very handy when the canoe is carried a very short distance right-side up; they also make ideal fastening points for the painters and for lines to secure the canoe fore and aft when it is on the roof racks. For lining or towing the canoe, the ends of a "Y"-shaped bridle may also be attached to these thwarts and joined to a single line underneath the canoe's prow, providing lift below the waterline. This is a much safer method of rigging than simply running lines from the canoe's deck, which can easily result in a capsizing. Finally, the little crosspieces have a structural function, helping the decks hold the gunwales together up in the ends and taking much of the stress off the deck screws. These are all good enough reasons for installing the little thwarts, which add very little weight to the canoe.

Brass or copper half-oval stembands are really the only acceptable hardware for dressing up the ends of a wood-canvas canoe. Those with a concave-shaped contact surface are especially suited because the canvas seam rests inside the groove and the bands sit squarely on the stem.

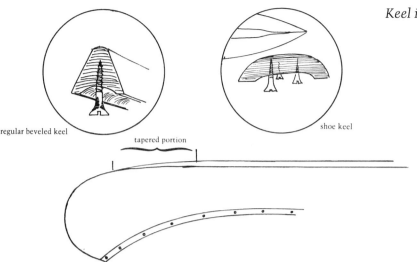

Keel installation.

regular beveled keel   tapered portion   shoe keel

After being pre-drilled and countersunk, they are held in place by ¾" No. 4 brass wood screws. I taper the trailing end to a feather edge to prevent it from catching on things when it is being beached, and fit the other end right up underneath the protruding gunwales. On more typical canoes, whose decks and gunwales end flush with the face of the stem, the stemband is brought up past the deck a few inches, then folded over and fastened to the top of the deck. Unless the canoe has a keel, you will not want the length of the stemband to exceed that of the stem inside. Before I fasten this one, I fill the concave surface with bedding compound. I also dip each of the screws in the compound before inserting them, because these are the only through-hull fastenings other than the little tacks covered with filler, and the most common cause of leaking.

Keels are common fixtures on most wood canoes; they help the canoe track on flatwater, and provide a lot of protection to the bottom of the canoe. Most river paddlers shun them because they inhibit the canoe's ability to slide laterally when a draw stroke is applied, and they can catch on rocks and ledges that a smooth-bottomed canoe would slide over easily. When a keel is installed on a river canoe it is usually the wide, flat shoe style — 2" or 2 ½" wide and only ½" or ⅝" deep. The ends of a shoe keel taper in width as well as depth towards the ends, fairing into the entry of the canoe. Standard keels are cut from ⅞"-square stock and are beveled on both sides to a width of ⅜" or ½" on the face. Unless there is a wooden outside stem on the canoe to which the keel is mated, is is also tapered in depth over the final 2' down to about 3/16" at the end which is normally at the start of the stem's curve. The keel may also be tapered gently in width until the end matches the width of the stemband, which is run up and over the tapered portion of

The finished product should justify all the care and expense that has gone into its construction. GC

A pleasing appearance and responsive performance are the real rewards for careful workmanship.

the keel. Metal bands running the entire length of the keel are a needless addition of considerable weight.

Most keels are hollowed out along the contact surface to hold bedding compound before they are installed on the canoe. This can be done by running the keel past a shaper or router fitted with the proper bit, or with the table saw with the blade set very shallow (about ¼") and the keel run over the blade at an angle defined by an improvised wooden fence. Unless the keel is to be kept bright, is is best installed before the canoe is painted. A pair of chalk lines to define the keel's position exactly is a requirement, and it is helpful to have a second person holding the keel down against the bottom exactly in place while the builder crouches beneath the overturned canoe with the drill, using the garboard seam as a reference for the centerline of the canoe. Even though the keel's groove is filled with bedding compound, each screw is dipped in the sealer before being driven. Most of the screws are fastened from the inside on every other rib, and appropriate finish washers are employed to prevent the heads from burrowing too deeply into the cedar rib surfaces. The tapered portions at the ends — that run along the stem — are fastened from the outside through the planking and into the stem inself. The keel is painted along with the canoe, and the seam sealed by the paint. With the polished stembands in place and the excess bedding compound cleaned up with mineral spirits and a soft rag, I turn my attention to first cleaning then lightly sanding the gunwales and thwarts with 400-grit paper. They will need to be refreshed after the masking and painting processes, and will take the most abuse in the ensuing years. Spreading on the spar varnish is the final bit of attention I will lavish on this canoe. I am like the schoolmaster who has devoted a period of time to the development of a student, and am now imparting a final lecture summing up the essense of the lessons I have delivered to him over the years. I would wonder if I had properly prepared him for all that lies ahead — all the twists and trials and traps that may lurk along his path. All I can hope for is that the advice has been on the average sound, and the preparation as thorough as possible under the circumstances. Let's at least hope I have instilled in the student the spirit of self-reliance.

That is all I can wish for with the canoe also. It hasn't a will of its own, but the validity of the design, quality of the materials, and integrity of my craftmanship add up to a kind of spirit that can lift the canoe through challenges with a style that will surprise and delight its owner.

7

Canoe Repair
and Restoration

"Can you repair this canoe? Is it worth it?" These are the first questions a person asks as I stare up into the darkened spaces of a canoe upside down on a car rack. The first question is easy to answer! "Yes I can repair it." Given one rib, I could build a canoe around it — that's no problem. The determining factor is how much this person is willing to spend, which relates to the second question. I can't really say if it's worth it or not. That is a personal decision that the owner must make. Is the owner interested in the historical significance of the wooden canoe or is he looking for an investment? I do know that if a person is looking for monetary return on his investment, he would have better luck with pork bellies. Occasionally, the right canoe in the right place will meet the right customer but that is a rarity. In most cases the seller will make back what he has invested in a professionally resotred canoe, but the market does not generally supply much of a profit. If a person is interested in the canoe because of its history, and appreciates the characteristics of a wooden canoe, it's only a matter of what he can afford, unless he is able to the restoration himself.

Most of the wooden canoes that have been presented to me to be examined were originally high-quality canoes, otherwise they would not have lasted as long as they have. With luck the manufacturer of the canoe is known, which helps determine its historic value. Many unidentified canoes are quality craft, but many people unfortunately equate quality with name recognition. Generally, the older canoes have a style, design, and quality that sets them apart from any of the canoes found in today's mass market. Their grace and beauty is appreciated by almost everyone, and while it is true an older canoe will never be as strong and flexible as a new wooden canoe, it can be made perfectly serviceable for 75 percent of all recreational canoeing uses.

Quality materials for making repairs are not easy to locate, and they tend to be expensive, but a canoe is a relatively small item and large quantities of materials are

FOR SALE: Quality wooden canoe, needs some work. Priced to move.

seldom needed. By far, the largest expense is labor. Many amateurs do outstanding restorations on their canoes, but not without a considerable expense of time. The bigger the job, the more woodworking skills will be required but as with most jobs, persistence pays off and given time and patience and a little care, most difficulties that a canoe can present can be overcome.

A Careful Survey

I always try to make a distinction between repair and restoration. Repairs to me are jobs that can be accomplished with a minimum of fuss, don't take long, and don't substantially alter the condition of the craft. Restorations are much larger projects that physically renew the entire craft. Trying to do a repair job on a craft that requires restoration is a waste of time and money. There is no sense in replacing one rib when five more are broken, patching canvas that is 30 years old, or varnishing over six coats of old varnish. It's much better to let an old canoe die a dignified death lying in the shade of a cedar tree than to beat it to death with makeshift repairs, just trying to make it float one more time.

The canoe that I'm working on is a 1897 E.H. Gerrish, built in Bangor, Maine. Gerrish was the world's first commercial wood-and-canvas canoe builder, so it adds a special sense of history to the project. The canoe has been passed from father to son, not used very hard, always stored out of the weather, and has had reasonable care most of the time — but still suffers from benign neglect. The only visible damage other than the obvious need for new canvas is one broken inwale, four or five broken ribs, and some damaged planking where it has recently been dropped on the corner of some object.

The rail system is of the old closed-gunwale construction, and I anticipate the top and outside railcaps will have a certain amount of rot on their enclosed surfaces. Also, the ends of the caps, at the stems, have been broken off and/or cracked, so I assume I will have to replace all four caps. Sighting down the rails everything looks fair except for the one obvious break, but when I place some inward pressure on the rail, the sections between the thwarts move independently of each other, indicating that both inwales are broken at the bolt holes but their breaks are hidden by the caps.

There are many coats of old, dark varnish on the interior, making it hard to detect any but the most seriously broken ribs. I look down the outside of the hull to see if there are any humps or bulges that would indicate more broken ribs, but everything looks smooth and fair. By pressing in on the outside of the hull and watching the ribs inside flex, I can spot several more breaks. The most common areas for breaks are the center of the canoe and around the seats. I can now count at least 10 broken ribs. Generally, I assume there are about 20 to 25 percent more broken ribs than I can spot right away. Given the Gerrish's age, I feel safe in assuming that at least five to ten more ribs will need replacing. No one wants to believe that his canoe is going to need 15 to 20 new ribs when all he can see are five broken ones, but it's better to assume too many than not enough. I finally had to replace 18 ribs — a lot of ribs to replace but since the shape of the hull is in good conditioin, I'll be able to use the hull as a form on which to bend the new ribs. If the hull was distorted, it would be a considerably more difficult project.

An examination of the deck and stems does not reveal anything until I poke my head under the decks. That is where I find him, the resident spider (*Canoest spiderest Americanes*) and his family. He normally will drop onto my head or glasses. I don't know how they do it but even after I tear this canoe apart, and completely clean, paint, and varnish it, the spider and his family will still be there. They are seldom lethal so I just continue poking around. A sharp awl poked into the bottom of the deck and the stems fails to show any soft spots except for the top of one stem. The sound stem, however, is broken in two spots so it will have to be competely replaced.

The seat frames and thwarts are all in good shape even though they move around a lot, indicating their bolt holes are very worn. The ends will have to be resored and the seats recaned.

One last look down the center of the canoe when it is sitting right side up determines if it has been twisted out of shape. I sight down the two peaks of the stems and imagine a line down the center of the canoe. If the two stems and the center of the canoe don't line up I know the hull is twisted, which adds to the difficulty. Fortunately, everything is still straight. The planking appears in good condition, and it looks like I will have to replace more planking due to working on the rails and stems than due to the actual breaks and cracks.

The preliminary investigation takes only about a half-hour, and now I can add up what is to be done:

1. Replace inwale and caps
2. Remove old varnish, recondition, and revarnish
3. Replace one stem and splice the tip of the other
4. Recane seats
5. Recondition thwarts and seat frames
6. Replace 15-20 ribs
7. Replace 50 linear feet of planking
8. Recanvas and paint

Even with my cautious estimates I know that I can be caught by surprise by some undetected development, so I always look forward to the time I can dig into the canoe and find out if my estimates were correct. Within a couple of hours I'll have the canvas off and a good idea if the project is going to be more difficult than I expect.

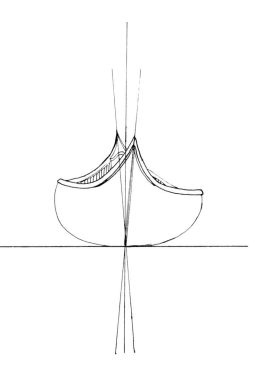

Sighting down canoe to see if it's twisted out of shape.

Ripping and Tearing, Prying and Pulling

As in most jobs, before I can start on the canvas several extraneous items have to be attended to. First, the brass stembands, outside wooden stems, and the outside railcaps must be removed. Metal stembands don't wear out often, but it's very difficult to remove them without breaking them. If the heads of the screws are not worn off, it is a simple matter of unscrewing them. Many times the bands have been painted and the paint has to be scraped off to find the screws, and then a sharp awl can be used to dig out the slot for the screwdriver. If the head of the screw is stripped, I resort to prying up the end of the band and run a hacksaw blade beneath the band and cut off the screws. The old bedding compound may make it seem like the band is glued on, but gentle prying will lift it off. If the band comes off in one piece, it can be scraped and sanded and made to look just like new but I wouldn't bother reusing a broken band. The outside stem is screwed to the inside stem from the outside. The heads of the screws will be exposed once the stemband is off. If I'm lucky, the screws are brass or bronze instead of corroded steel. If the screws won't come

Gerrish Canoe Company

Evan (Eve) H. Gerrish started building wood-canvas canoes in Bangor as early as 1875, becoming the world's first manufacturer of wood-canvas canoes. Gerrish's business grew steadily over a 30-year period from a one-man shop producing fly rods, snowshoes, and other sporting equipment to a modest-sized factory producing hundreds of canoes. Eve Gerrish always remained active in the construction of the canoes, and his catalogs emphasized his guiding experience and the availability of accommodations at his "comfortable" camps at B Pond near his home town of Brownville.

In 1882, he had hired his first employee and was selling canoes for about $25 each. By 1890 he had a new 40x50' two-story factory built on the corner of French and Hancock streets in Bangor. Production had risen to over 60 canoes a year with six employees. His advertisements boasted of customers as far away as Montana and North Carolina, with train carloads going to the recreational market on the Charles River in Massachusetts. By 1895 there were many canoe builders in the state and Gerrish was reported to be the largest, producing over 150 canoes annually, average price $45, with 10 employees. Gerrish had sent canoe exhibits to the New Orleans World's Fair, where his exhibit won a gold medal, and the Columbian Exposition.

Eve Gerrish advanced the construction, style, and design of his canoes throughout his proprietorship. He helped introduce 30' war canoes that were very popular with canoe clubs, as well as motor canoes, and offered the new style of open-gunwale canoe as early as 1905.

A small rectangular 2-½x1" copper tag on the forward deck, stamped with E.H. Gerrish, Maker, Bangor, Maine, identified his canoes. Unfortunately, he did not apply a serial number or otherwise date his canoes, which makes it difficult to determine the age of the few surviving craft. The canoes reflect the typical graceful shape of the Penobscot and Malecite bark canoes. The seats, thwarts, and decks are finely proportioned, unlike the heavier styles which would become popular in later years.

Gerrish had hoped that his only child, Stanley, would take over the canoe

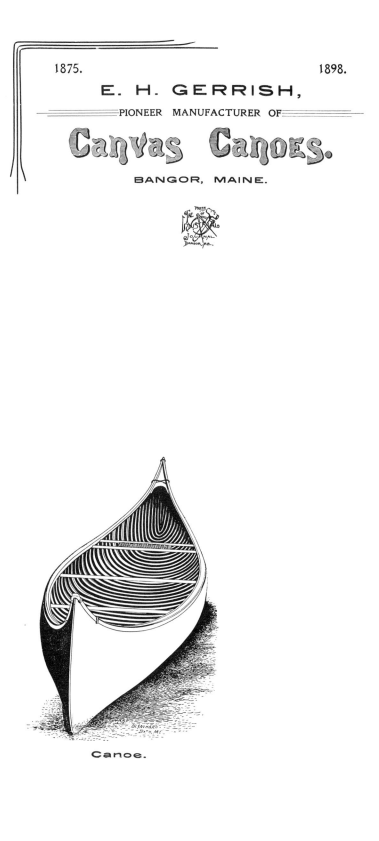

1875.   1898.

E. H. GERRISH,

PIONEER MANUFACTURER OF

Canvas Canoes.

BANGOR, MAINE.

Canoe.

Row Boat.

company but instead the boy obtained advanced degrees in chemistry and chose to follow that field. By 1909 Eve Gerrish was 61 years old and sold the business to Herbert D. Walton, who for several years had been his general manager. Eve and his wife continued to live in Bangor until 1919, when they moved back to Brownville. He continued to operate his camps at B Pond until his death in January, 1930 at the age of 82.

One year afer he bought the company, Herbert Walton moved it up-river to his home town of Cardville (Costigan). Herbert employed his two brothers and for at least a few years the shop remained a going concern. Gerrish had developed a rowing canoe that was very popular in the salmon pools of the Penobscot River and Walton appears to have expanded upon this craft, which was locally known as a "salmon peapod."

The Walton brothers did not stay together very long and the company had a rapid and steady decline in production throughout the '20s, when it was a one-man shop. A fire destroyed most of the shop in the early '30s, and Herbert quit canoe building altogether. Parts of the shop were still standing until 1978, when the area was bulldozed to build a new house. The only evidence of the shop was a copper tag found by the new owner in a nearby stone wall. It stated: "Gerrish Canoe Co - Costigan, Maine."

out, the hacksaw has to be worked under the wood stem and the screws cut off. It is surprising in how many hidden places even the best of the old canoe companies used steel or galvanized steel fastenings. Perhaps they used a much better grade steel than is available today because many of the fastenings are still doing their job, but others are corroded to almost nothing. They certainly make any repairs or restorations much more difficult.

This canoe does not have an outside keel or the standard screwed-on outside gunwale. If it did, I would continue with the awl and clean out the heads of the screws that held them in place. The majority of the screws for the keel are found on the inside of the canoe, imbedded in the ribs along the centerline of the bottom of the canoe. Usually they are fastened on every other rib. The very last foot or so on both ends of the keel is fastened from the outside, screwed through the keel into the end of the inside stem.

Removing the railcaps is not much of a problem since they are to be replaced — just rip and tear. Caps are usually difficult to get off in one piece; they are frail, and most of the time they're nailed on with very long, round-shank escutcheon pins, the heads of which are buried into the wood. A gentle prying and poking is all that can be done, and it takes time to get the cap off without destroying it. I save several sections of the caps so I can refer back to them when I make the new ones.

The canvas is tacked to the canoe along the rail under the railcap (or the outside gunwale) and along the face of the stems. Along the rails, the canvas and the tacks holding it can usually simply be pulled away without first removing the tacks. The canvas along the stem resists, but it can usually be pried off with a tack puller and screwdriver. Most of the time the canvas just pulls away from the stem tacks, leaving what appears to be hundreds of tiny corroded tack heads to be pulled out of the stem. Many times a tack-puller will just strip off the head of a tack imbedded in a hardwood stem, but a pair of pliers will pull it out.

With the canvas pulled away from the gunwale and the stem, the canvas will drop right off the hull. Now the naked canoe resembles a skinned animal. I always feel the canoe skin should be tacked onto the side of the shop like a raccoon skin in a Western movie, but I don't do it.

Depending on the tightness of the planking and where the canoe has been used, there may be a lot of sand imbedded in the hull that has worked in between the planking and the canvas. Brush it off using a brush — there may be some tack heads sticking up just enough to dig into a sweeping hand.

Half-inch reinforcing battens screwed to the broken inwale.

All this movement of the old hull and the removal of the caps causes the inwales to completely break at several of the weak spots that were detected earlier. As a temporary measure, just to keep the rails together until they can be replaced, I take a scrap batten ½"x1"x12' and screw it every 16" along the inside of the broken rail.

It should be an easy matter, unbolting the thwarts and seats, but I know the nuts on the steel bolts will be frozen with rust. The rail will be replaced so I dig out the top of the bolts and hold them with a pair of Vise Grip pliers to prevent them from turning. If it is not possible to dig with abandonment into the rail, the only other recourse is to cut off the bolt from underneath, a very awkward proposition.

All this ripping and tearing, prying and pulling may take four hours or more, depending on how careful I need to be. And then I reach a good time for standing back to see what condition the hull is in. The planking is smooth and flat, and only a very few areas show any damage or cracking. I'm always hoping I will find a message or a signature written on the hull, but today is not the day.

Stripping the Finish

On the average, the next job takes only about four hours, but stripping the old interior varnish is also the most unpleasant task in the whole restoration process. Anytime the varnish is checked with age or has multiple layers, it is a waste of time simply trying to sand the interior and revarnish. There is no way out of this smelly, unpleasant job, and I would gladly skip it if I could, but it must be done not just for the interior's appearance, but in order to expose the true condition of the ribs and planking, maybe revealing more breaks and splits. It also allows me to oil the interior to restore some flexibility to the ribs and planking.

There are many and various ways to strip old varnish and paint. Filling the canoe with a water and lye solution or even sandblasting has been used with success by some. The system I use is the most common: brushing on a water soluble liquid paste remover, scraping, scrubbing, and washing it off. The remover is available at hardware, paint, and discount stores. A high price does not indicate the best remover; I often use the most inexpensive remover from a discount store with very good results. There are so many different types of paints and varnishes used on canoes that no one remover works best on all canoes, and sometimes it's a guessing game trying to find the most effective remover before the canoe is completely stripped.

Rubber gloves, eye protection, an apron, a lot of cold, fresh water, and a well-ventilated space are requirements.

Applying the varnish remover.

The chemicals in the remover will burn bare skin and the fumes can be overpowering. All precautions printed on the remover can should be followed.

I'll start at one end of the canoe, slapping on enough remover to cover about one-quarter of the canoe. I use plenty of remover, two gallons overall. Neatness does not count, but volume of remover does — the more remover applied the better job it does. If the remover loses its shine or wet look, it means it is drying up and more remover must be applied. When the varnish bubbles up, it can be gently scraped away. For a scraper I use old, dull plane irons of various sizes. After I scrape once I apply another thick coating of remover over the complete interior, scrub with a coarse bronze wool pad, and wash the canoe out with a powerful garden hose. A long-handled brush and scraper will be needed to reach up into the stem areas. The best way I know to do this job is to have someone else do it. The noted canoe restorer in mid-state New York, Jack McGreivey, once employed a lady he referred to has his "stripper" who seemed to relish this work, but I haven't had his luck with employees or women.

Bleaching and Staining

Even with the old varnish removed the color of the wood may be very dark, stained in areas, or have a weathered gray appearance. While the canoe is still wet from rinsing, it is a good time to restore the wood's natural color. The basic technique is to wash out the canoe with some kind of bleach. I have used household bleach, and it took care of the stains but gave the wood a very pale, washed-out color. Eight ounces of oxalic acid mixed with three gallons of cold

Bleaching the old wood.

water is also a good bleach, but after using the remover I don't like working with any more harsh chemicals. I now use a cleaner that is advertised for teak decks on yachts. This two-part teak cleaner does a very good job restoring the cedar's natural color. It's easy to use, only takes about 30 minutes and doesn't seem to be very harsh on the skin or the lungs. The first part is brushed on, lightly scrubbed with a soft brush, then washed off. The second part is then brushed on and simply washed out. The color difference resulting from any bleach is always very dramatic, which means the whole canoe must be done or none of it. Trying to do just a small area results in a very spotty appearance.

New Rails

My next task is to replace the broken inwales. As with many older canoes, there is a considerable rise in the sheer at the ends of the rails, so I'm going to have to steam and pre-bend the gunwales. The tops of the ribs are very weak and need reconditioning before they can be refastened to the new rail. All these steps will be spaced over a three-day period. Given a canoe with rails that didn't have to be steamed, and rib ends that were in good shape, the whole operation of replacing inwales would take less than one day.

I cut out a small section of the canoe's gunwale to use as a sample to shape the new rails. The rails are shaped and tapered to match the originals, only they are made 2' longer. The extra length will make the bending process easier.

Before I put the rails in the tube, I marked them left and right because there is a bevel on the rib side of the rail and I don't want to fumble around with a hot rail trying to

New rails clamped under the old rail.
Spacers maintain the proper canoe width.

determine which side goes where. The 18" rails are placed in a 20'x4"-diameter pipe to be steamed. Only the last 6' of each end on the rails needs to be steamed, but by using the long pipe I'll be able to bend both ends with only one steaming operation. While the rails are steaming, I remove the top row of planking all the way around the canoe to allow access to the nails holding the old ribs and rail together. I let the rails steam for about one and a half hours; spruce doesn't bend very easily, and a few extra minutes won't hurt as long as the wood isn't over-cooked. Excessive steaming will actually make the bending more difficult.

Once the rail is pulled from the pipe there is not much time to bend it, maybe three minutes at the most. I don't need any special form or jig because I can bend the new rail right under the old one, inside the canoe. I make sure I have plenty of clamps and pads on hand, spread out within reach in the bottom of the canoe. I call Jerry over to help in the operation, since I wouldn't have time enough to do both ends myself.

When everything is all set, one rail is pulled out of the steam box, slid in through the opened-up bow of the canoe under the deck, and passed on to the other end until each end extends beyond the canoe about 12". Quickly, the middle of the gunwale is drawn toward the proper side and clamped under the old rail, then clamped once at the quarter, and again under the deck and on the ends. The extra length at the ends makes the rails easier to grab and bend up at the ends. Once the ends are clamped and in proper position, we go back and space clamps about every 18" the length of the rail. After both rails are in position, braces are placed in several spots to maintain the proper width of the hull.

If the Gerrish wasn't such an historic canoe and if the depth of the canoe wasn't already a shallow 11", I might have considered fastening the new rail right in place under the old one. It's a lot faster and easier, but that's not to be for ths canoe.

I let the new rails dry for a full day before I release them and begin removing the old rail. The tops of the ribs come to a featheredge at the top of the rail and are in very weak condition. Gerrish used three long steel nails on each rib, and it is difficult to work the ribs loose without destroying the tops of the ribs. When the old rails are off, I treat the top of each rib with a liquid epoxy that will soak into the cells of any softened or decayed wood fibers. A heavy paste epoxy is applied to those areas where the rib is split or broken. It will take another day before the epoxy will dry, and by then the rib tops will be hard and firm and strong enough to be nailed to the new rail. The canoe will be without any rails overnight, and right now it looks as though it could unfold itself and become a giant wooden floor mat. Since there are no rails to pull the canoe together, I wrap several lengths of rope around the hull to maintain the hull's proper shape. Small wooden blocks are placed around the top of the planking to keep the rope from

Repairing Rib Tops

Removing the old rail.

Installing a new inwale.

digging into the planking. It's surprising how fast a canoe will lose its shape without its thwarts, so any time the canoe is without them overnight, I make sure there is some measure of bracing to take their place.

It seems all I have done is rip and tear the canoe apart, but now with the installation of the new rails the whole project looks like the canoe might really come out of it alive instead of dying on the operating table. The inside faces of the ribs with the hardened epoxy are sanded smooth and the new rails fit nicely into positon. The gunwales have straightened out a bit overnight, but not so much I can't pull them back into shape. I redrill the ribs for ¾" No. 14 bronze ring nails and fasten them to the rail. Some of the broken ribs are skipped because they'll have to be taken out later, but there are too many to skip all of them —perhaps every other one. There is a lot of visual checking; I sight down the length of the rail to make sure it has a fair line and no humps or dips have developed from putting the rail on without the benefit of a form. The tops of the ribs aren't always in perfect alignment with each other, and any mistakes here will have a noticeable effect on the look of the finished canoe and should be corrected.

Removing Broken Ribs

Replacing the broken ribs seems to be at the heart of any restoration project no matter what other serious problems there are. Studying the cleaned-out hull, I can easily spot the original 10 broken ribs, and four more can also be seen. They are all marked with a red crayon inside and out so I won't make the mistake of removing a good rib by mistake, which has been known to happen. No matter how carefully I search I know I'll spot several more broken ribs before I'm done, and with the ribs that will break while bending I plan on cutting enough stock for about 20 to 22 ribs. Before the stock is cut, one of the broken ribs is removed to determine the rib's exact thickness, taper, and edge bevel. The whole operation of removing, shaping, steaming, bending, drying, replacing, sanding, and staining will take place over a three- or four-day period. If there were only a couple of ribs to be replaced it could be done in a matter of hours, but with this many ribs extra precautions have to be taken to insure the canoe maintains its original shape.

I've removed ribs by every method except nuclear bomb, and I would probably try that if I could get an E.P.A. permit. The big problem is removing the clinched tack without destroying the good planking while prying out the tacks. Using a disc grinder on the inside of the rib to grind off the clinched part of the tack and then pulling out the remain-

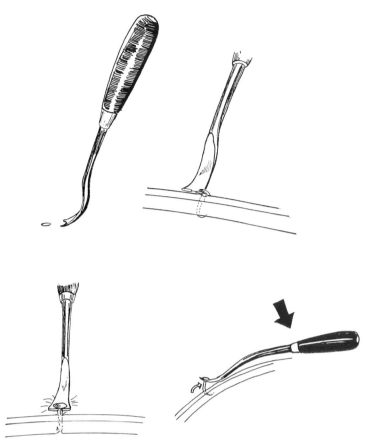

Removing a tack: Lift the head of the tack with the corner of the puller. Do not pull it straight out, but roll it out so the clinched end does not tear the wood.

Taking out the old rib by removing all fastenings and pulling the rib toward the center of the canoe.

ing straight section of the tack works well, even if it's quite a dusty job. Splitting the rib apart with a chisel and then snipping off the clinched portion of the tacks with wire cutters will achieve the same results but is a little slower. Both methods are very effective but in most cases the easiest, fastest, and most effective method is the direct pulling of the tacks from the outside with great care and finesse. A good tack-puller is required for cleanly digging out the buried tack head and for the proper prying out of the clinched part of the tack, but a frontal assault on the tack will result in a large crater of destroyed planking. A couple of craters aren't anything to worry about, but a row of them along the length of each rib would be a serious problem. Each builder jealously guards his personally modified tack-puller. I know Jerry can't stand mine and I can't use his — at least not without a few condescending comments of proper tool design. The pullers are regular commercially available ones, modified to our own tastes. The fat ends have been filed down and tapered to a fine edge, and we've bent the shafts for better prying action. I had a student who used what looked like a mini 6″ crowbar; I laughed when I first saw it, but much to my chagrin he had very good results with it, proving it's more a factor of care taken than of exact design.

Just the corner or tip of the puller is forced under the lip of the tack head to pry it up just enough so the face of the puller will fit under the complete head of the tack. The tack can now be pried up, but it is not pulled straight out. The tack has to be pulled or rolled to one side so that the clinched part of the tack will *slide* out of the nail hole instead of ripping its way through the rib and planking. There is no one correct direction to pry up, so the tack is rocked to the left and right, back and forth, until the direction of least resistance can be determined, and then it can be pried and rolled in that direction.

Gerrish's tacks are made of copper and are a bit blunter and fatter than the finely shaped brass tacks that have been in use since the 1920s. His tacking pattern is interesting in that the tacks are set in diagonal rows across the width of the ribs, three tacks per plank spaced every inch apart. The diagonals are sloped from the center of the canoe down toward their respective stems. All other canoe manufacturers' patterns I have seen have alternated each tack from left to right, except for one. Several years ago Jerry announced he had discovered a diagonal tacking pattern that made the plank lay on the ribs better than the alternating method. At first, I thought he was trying to blow smoke at me, much like his tack-puller design, but it did seem to be effective. Now I can see this technique was used by an historic builder and simply forgotton over the years until Jerry rediscoveered it by trial and error.

Installing New Ribs

Stock 60" long is ripped out for the ribs and shaped for thickness and width. If the ribs do not taper in width, then the length of the rib is unimportant as long as it's long enough. The Gerrish does have a taper, so the length of each rib will have to be measured over the outside of the hull, the new rib cut to that length plus 2", the center marked on the back of the rib, the taper cut on each end, the bevel shaped on the sides, and then everything sanded smooth.

All the ribs are steamed at the same time in my small steam box. I'll use the hull as a form and bend the ribs exactly as described in the building chapter. There isn't a strongback to hold down the center of the rib, so it if it's needed I'll use a stick braced from the ceiling to the top of the rib to force it down. I normally bend the new rib one rib closer to the stem of the canoe than where the broken rib is located. This allows for the difference in the fullness of the outside of the canoe as opposed to the inside shape. At the center of the canoe I may place the new rib three or four

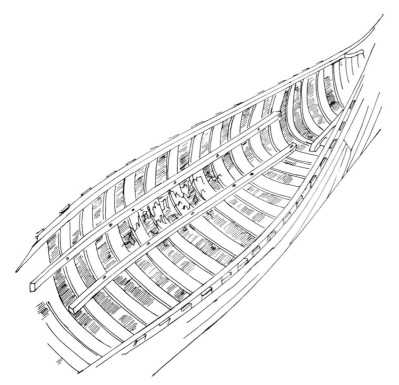

Battens are screwed to the inside of the canoe to regain the proper hull shape before replacement ribs are bent over the outside of the canoe.

Using the canoe as a form to bend replacement ribs.

ribs ahead to get the proper difference of fullness. Near the stem, where there is a dramatic difference in the hull shape, I may place the new rib only a half rib forward of the broken rib.

The ribs are bent one at a time after steaming for about 20 minutes. The center of the rib that has been marked is placed along the hull's centerline, the top brace is put into position, and then one end is bent at a time and clamped to the inwale. Holding the rib down in place, adjusting the clamp, and holding the pad on the inwale so that it won't be marked up takes about three hands or a lot of fingers. If the strength in the fingers holding the rib weakens, and if the repairer is standing in line with the rib, then WHAP, the rib will spring out and hit him in the face — not exactly deadly, but unpleasant, nevertheless.

I'm lucky that the hull is not deformed, and I am able to bend ribs wherever they are needed. If the hull was deformed I could bend the ribs at their respective places on the other end of the canoe. Another method is to screw some battens to the inside of the hull to force the hull back into its proper position. The battens extend past the deformed area by several feet and will either pull or push the deformed section into its proper alignment. Screw holes in the good ribs won't be serious, and the tips of the screws that project through the hull can be filed or ground down if they are in the way.

When there are but one or two ribs to be bent, I don't bother to heat up the steamer. I simply boil a couple of quarts of water, wrap the rib in a towel, and pour the boiling water over the towel. Immediately the rib and towel are bent over the hull, taken off, the towel is removed, and then the rib is put back on the hull and clamped into its proper position. I'm always embarrassed to use this primitive method, but it is very effective. (Insulated rubber gloves are necessary because boiling water will run off the towel onto your hands.)

Never remove and replace two consecutive ribs at the same time. When a new rib is put into place, it seldom fits perfectly without a certain amount of pressure to make it seat itself flat against the planking. Too much pressure in an area of weak planking will cause the hull to bulge out. It is very difficult not to cause a bulge when a section has a long series of broken ribs, so this calls for great care and attention to the placement of each rib. The Gerrish has several spots with four broken ribs in a row, not the worst situation, but it could prove difficult.

When nailing in the new rib a single section of old broken planking that is to be replaced can be skipped over, but if there is a lot of broken planking much of it will have to be temporarily fastened to the new rib to provide the plank support for the other ribs to be replaced. The fastening is not as easy as on a new canoe because there is no form with steel bands to hammer against. I press about 15 tacks into the hull with my thumb, and lightly tap them with the hammer so they won't fall out. Then, holding the clinching iron on the inside, I drive the tacks home. Several of the tacks that didn't have very good holds will fall out from all the vibration of the clinching, and they'll have to be re-

When a series of new ribs needs to be forced into positon, battens are used to reinforce the hull so that the replacement ribs don't make bulges in the planking.

A new rib that has been bent, shaped, sanded, and stained; now it's ready to be fastened.

A good helper holding the clinching iron can make clinching the center part of the canoe easier.

This clinching iron is heavy enough so that it doesn't have to be held. It's handy for the hard-to-reach center of the canoe, but not so helpful in the stem!

placed. The Gerrish will require over 600 tacks, which makes for one sore thumb. There's none of the fancy spitting out of tacks from a full mouth and driving them home with a series of solid hammer blows which Jerry gets to enjoy on a new canoe. If an assistant can be found to hold the clinching iron, it will make the job much easier. My young son has become quite adept at sitting in a canoe and holding the iron while I lie on my back under the canoe driving the tacks home. He knows the sound of a solid Thump when the hammer and iron are in correct alignment instead of a hollow, vibrating Womp when the iron is not properly backing up the hammer blows.

About this time other broken ribs will become evident, and a second steaming will be necessary. I try to let the ribs dry overnight on the hull before I install them, but in a pinch a three- or four-hour drying period is sufficient. It is a good time to stain the rib before the rib is nailed into position. A new rib in an old canoe will stick out like my sore thumb. As with most jobs, this staining is not as straightforward as it would first appear. The proper color can seldom be picked right off the shelf. Matching the color of the old wood to the new is not good enough. Later, when the hull is oiled and then varnished, the old wood color will change to a much darker shade but the new wood won't. Proper matching can be a time-consuming process. The best method is the long process of sanding, oiling, and varnishing pieces of old rib and planking stock to see what the finish color will be. Stain different colors on samples of new wood, then oil and varnish then to see which is the best match. Many times stains have to be mixed to obtain the proper color. This whole process might take several days, so it is best to start the process long before it is needed. I normally use a mix of Minwax oil stains. Their Old Colonial stains seem to come close in most cases, but I usually add a little Golden Oak, Pine, or Gray Driftwood for the proper color. I've also used Kiwi brown and dark brown shoe polish and stove blacking as the situation requires. Ribs and planking do not always take the same stain, even if they are the same type of wood. Many times the ribs and planking were sawn out differently, and even though from the same species won't accept the stain the same. The pre-stained ribs can get beaten up a little before it is time to varnish, but it's a simple matter to touch them up as required. Staining the whole canoe is never the answer because the old and new wood will not accept the stain uniformly, and there would still be a noticeable difference in their colors.

Now my attention is directed towards the stems. The broken stem reveals a second break and working the stem and its steel fastening loose from the planking is quite difficult. The ends of the planking have taken quite a beating, but an application of liquid epoxy will restore most of them; still, some will have to be cut back four or five ribs and new planking installed. I'll have to make a custom form to bend the new stem over, so before I take the stem apart I take a large piece of cardboard and hold it next to the stem and trace off the curve. This curve is cut out and held up to the face of the stem, the high spots are trimmed down, and extra sections of cardboard are added to span any low spots. After a good pattern is made, the curve is traced onto a section of ½" plywood. This is the outside curve of the stem, but the new stem has to be bent to the inside curve which has a smaller or tighter radius. The stem is ⅞" thick, so a curve can be drawn ⅞" inside the outside curve. This would give the shape the stem is to be bent to, but the hardwood stem will have a tendency to spring back or straighten itself out after it is taken off the form. A curve drawn 1-¼" inside the outside curve will give a shpae that is a bit tighter and will compensate for the springback in the new stem. The curve is also extended several inches beyond the actual end of the final stem. The plywood form is now cut out and the curve is faired and sanded smooth. Some ¾" pine or spruce scraps are screwed to one side and then carved down to fit the curve. This will make the edge of the form 1-¼" thick, so it will be easy for

Making a pattern of the stem.

Bending a stem over a temporary form.

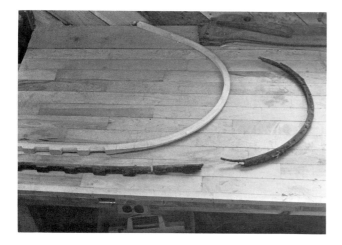

Shaping the new stem using the old one as a pattern.

Fitting a splice on a stem.

Using a press with solid forms is a good way to bend decks.

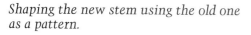

the ¾"-wide stem to rest against it. Two large holes are drilled in the form to accommodate the clamps that will hold the stems fast. On the Gerrish, the bottom of the stem is 1-½" wide and tapers to ⅞" wide about halfway up. Most stems are ¾" or ⅞" square before they are beveled. The new stem should be a couple of inches long on each end to allow for some play when it is finally put in place. The extra length also makes the stem easier to hold and bend over the form.

The garboard planks over the old stem are removed so the fastenings from the ribs into the stem can be removed. The old stem can be used as a pattern to notch the new one. Each stem is notched for the ribs a little bit differently, and the stem notches from one end of the canoe cannot be used as a pattern for the other end. When the stem is bevelled and notched, it should fit right in place over the ribs. A little work with a rasp should take care of any improper fits. The stem can be clamped to the ribs and new fastenings installed through the ribs. With its curve following the shape of the old planking, the stem is butted under the tip of the deck.

The tip of the other stem on this Gerrish is decayed and a fairly simple splice is all that is needed. About three or four rows of planking will have to be cut back for 2-4' on one side of the stem to expose and provide access. A long, angled cut is made across the old stem about 2-3" below the last section of rot. A section of ash 1" wide and long enough to form a pocket for the stem is shaped and beveled at the same angle as the stem. The splice is glued and held in position with two 1" No.4 bronze screws. The outside face of the old stem has been pocked by the old canvas tacks and shows the first signs of softness, so the whole stem is treated with the liquid epoxy. When the epoxy is dry the face of the stem can be sanded down about ¹⁄₃₂" to ¹⁄₁₆" to make a new, smooth, rot-resistant surface to which the new canvas is tacked.

Both decks on the Gerrish are in very good shape. They are small and narrow compared to decks on more modern canoes. I usually plan on at least renewing the tips of the decks, one of the most common areas of rot. To replace the tip, a long, tapered bevel is cut on the bottom of the deck. An oversize piece of matching wood is glued and screwed to the bevel, then the tip of the deck is carved out of the new section. A small, curved deck can be carved from a single thick piece of wood. The 20"-long decks as found on the Old Town Otca models have to be steamed and bent over a form. The decks are relatively short sections of wood, which make them hard to bend. A ladder-type jig isn't durable enough for this job, so I use a modified cider press to bend the deck between two large, carved blocks of wood. A pair of pipe clamps on either side of the blocks would work as well, but they are difficult to handle. I've never done it, but gluing three ¼"-thick sections of wood and pressing them in the jig would provide a perfectly usable laminated deck. A small coaming over the wide end of the deck would cover up the laminates, and no one would know it was not solid wood.

The planking on the Gerrish is all vertical-grain white cedar, and it's in very good condition. Even so, I have had to remove a considerable amount just to expose the rails and stems in order to work on them. I had to remove the top row of planking (sheerstrake), 6' of planking on the bottom of one stem (garboard strake), and miscellaneous planks along the tops of both stems. That makes 60' of planking plus another 20' of damaged planking, for a total of 80 linear feet of 3" planking to be replaced — or about a third of the total.

Widths of 3-4" are the most common for planking, however, it seems that each canoe varies. The usual thickness is 5/32", but that changes also. A slight difference of even 1/32" in the planking thickness will make a noticeable difference in the smoothness of the hull, so care must be taken to

A "ladder" jig can be used to bend decks or rails. There should be more crosspieces than shown here; they help obtain a smooth curve.

An oversized block is glued to the deck and will be carved down to form its new tip.

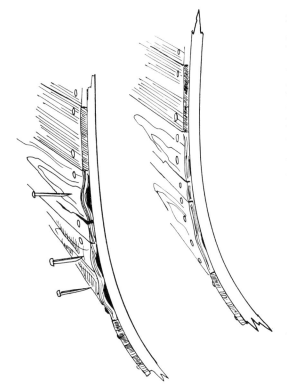

Flat-sawn planking that has buckled and split; the straight-grained planking remains in good condition.

reproduce the exact thickness. Many of the older canoes are planked with western red cedar. Red cedar is more brittle than white cedar but in most cases it is in very good condition because of the vertical grain. Vertical-grain planks and ribs shrink and swell evenly in all directions and are very stable. The much more commonly available flat-sawn planking does not expand or contract evenly, causing the plank to buckle and crack between the fastenings. In my region, red cedar is expensive and difficult to obtain so I usually replace it with the more flexible white cedar matched for grain and stained to match in color.

In addition to the obvious areas of damaged planking, I'm also looking for planking that is split, buckled, or cracked. Occasional splits can be repaired by tacking both side of the split for its entire length. Buckled planking usually is caused by a bad selection of wide, flat-grain planking or by spacing the tacks too far apart. Tacks should be spaced no more than an inch apart. The addition of more tacks to help flatten out the buckled plank will decrease the size of the buckle, but instead of one big buckle there will be several smaller ones.

As a rule, planking splices should be spaced at least three ribs apart and splices on the same rib kept apart at least three rows of planking, but there are acceptable alternatives. Replacement planks can be as short as 12″ or just a small 1x4″ patch. The number of splices and the condition of the original planking is more important than size and length. A hull in good condition with a lot of full-length planking would not be adversely affected by two splices next to one another. On the other hand, if there are already a lot of splices in the hull I might remove several extra feet of planking in order to space the splices farther apart.

The planking is removed by cutting it out with a sharp knife; care must be taken to cut only the planking and not the rib beneath. Bevel-lapped butt joints are nice but not really necessary on canoes that already have straight butt joints. Hot water may be required to help the plank take any bends and keep it from splitting when nailed. In fitting a new plank, the edges should not be tight against the other planks. It may look nice for awhile but later, after it gets wet, it will buckle or crack. To fit tapered or gored planks, an oversized replacement plank can be held on the outside of the hull over the space of the missing plank and the shape traced off onto the new plank from the inside. Fastening the plank is another three-handed job, clinching iron in one, hammer in another, and a third holding the plank in position. It's not too difficult when the plank lies flat but when it has to be curved as in the bilge area, there is no easy way to hold down the plank. Good hip and knee action help.

Removing a large area of damaged planking.

Sometimes the shape of the new plank can be traced from the old, broken plank.

A general review of the hull now will reveal areas where the old tacks were nailed too close to the edge or end of the plank, causing the wood to break away from the tack. There also will be places where the planking edges are lifted off the ribs. Tacks that are loose are evident by tack heads projecting above the hull. New tacks should be added to those areas. Old, loose tacks seldom reclinch satisfactorily and they should be removed. A good paint job on the finished canoe begins with a smooth hull, and close attention now will make the filling and painting that much easier. Once I'm satisfied that the hull is as smooth as it can be, all the tacks are securely clinched, and the planking is in good shape, I lightly sand the hull's exterior to clean the hull and to smooth away any plank edges that may stick up. I have to keep reminding myself the planking is only ⁵/₃₂" thick and that the factory already sanded it once, so I can't grind away with abandon with the disc or belt sander to achieve the ideal smooth hull. Dirt, sand, oil, varnish, and varnish remover residue will clog the sandpaper, but it's worth the extra sheets or belts to clean and smooth the hull as much as is feasible.

A vibrator sander with a rubber pad works the best for sanding the curved interior of the hull. Rib edges can only be smoothed by hand-sanding, being careful not to rub across the grain of the planking. The planking may be a bit rough from the varnish remover, but it is almost impossible to sand it in the direction of the grain because the ribs are in the way. Going across the grain with coarse sandpaper will leave deep scratches that will appear much worse when the canoe is varnished. If the planking must be sanded, a very light sanding across the grain with 150-grit or finer sandpaper will knock down most of the raised wood grain with a minimum of scratches.

The complete hull is vacuumed and cleaned and I take a last look for broken ribs, cracked planking, and loose tacks. I then apply a very generous coat of hot (not boiling) boiled linseed oil and clear Cuprinol wood preservative — three-quarters oil, one-quarter preservative. About two quarts will do the inside and outside of the hull. Neatness does not count on its application, only that everything receive a generous coating. The oil soaks into the wood fibers, minimizing the absorption of water later on and restoring some of the wood's flexibility. I heat the oil over a woodstove; I've never had it catch on fire, but I certainly watch it very closely. Hot oil splashed on the skin is not pleasant, so leather gloves are handy. I used to think that this would be a good job for one of the wide selection of cheap plastic bristle brushes that I have somehow obtained through the years. I didn't want to use a good varnish brush for this sloppy job, and a brush with paint in it would leach the paint into the oil and the canoe's interior. My shop is now decorated with several modern impressionistic brushes of sculptured melted plastic. An old, natural-bristle varnish brush is a much better choice of brush for the hot oil.

The oil is left to soak in overnight, and any excess oil that hasn't been absorbed by then is wiped off. The canoe can be canvased soon after that but since the interior is to be varnished, the inside must have at least four weeks of good drying atomosphere before it can be varnished. Since it takes the canvas filler about the same time to dry, the waiting period is no problem.

Reconditioning the ends of the thwarts and seats isn't very difficult or time consuming. The bolt holes are very worn and most of them have broken out the end of the wood, I drill out the hole with a slightly larger bit and then glue in a wooden plug. A wood shim is glued in place at the ends where the wood has broken away, and a 2″ No.8 bronze screw is screwed into the end of the thwart to keep it form

A wooden shim is glued on the broken end of a thwart.

The railcaps are pre-bent on a plywood form.

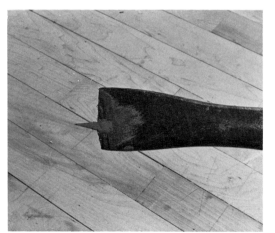

splitting apart again. Old thwarts are used as a pattern for replacements. Beat-up and dented thwarts can be taken down to good wood with a spokeshave, then sanded to look as good as new.

The canvasing, filling, and varnishing is exactly the same as for a new canoe. Instead of the regular outside gunwales, the Gerrish canoe has thin narrow caps on the outside and top. It would seem that the caps would be small enough to bend without steaming, but they aren't. The shape of the sheer for its first 4-5' is cut out on a piece of plywood, the cap is steamed, and the end of the cap can be clamped to the plywood to obtain the proper curve. The outside gunwale for the open-gunwale canoes are much stonger than the closed-gunwale caps. The rabbet on the open gunwale is a good place for rot to start, so I apply a coat of clear preservative along with some liquid epoxy to any areas that show signs of softness. The tips of the gunwales are generally in poor shape, either from dry rot or

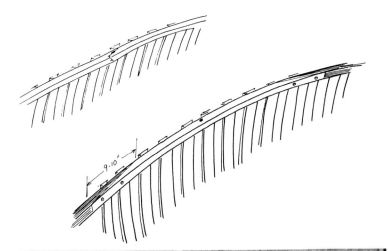

A long splice is needed for this broken rail.

The completely restored 1897 Gerrish canoe.

Recanvasing Sponsons

The strip-planked air chambers called sponsons, developed early in the century by several manufacturers to make their canoes unswampable, were very effective in their function, but surely complicate matters for anyone planning to preserve them when they recanvas their heirloom canoe. They were built right on the boat or canoe after the hull had been canvased and filled. Although there were variations in construction, the most common variety are D-shaped in cross section with a rather flattened top; they are fastened from the interior of the hull, the screws passing through the rib, planking, and canvas into the solid cross sections that provide the framework for the long strips. The sponsons are easy to remove as a unit, canvas and all, but if they require recanvassing themselves, the best procedure is to do it right on the canoe as it was done in the factories.

Once the hull has been canvassed and filled in the usual manner, a length of canvas 6" longer at each end and about 2-½' wide is stretched by hand along the sheerline and lightly tacked in place. About a third of the width is folded so it lies inside the canoe, and the remainder drapes down along the canoe's topsides. The screws holes are located and the naked sponson secured back into its original position. The lower flap of canvas is stretched up around the sponson and tacked every 3-4" along the upper outside corner of the sponson and then trimmed. The upper flap is stretched across the top of the sponson, overlapping the first, tacked along the same edge, neatly trimmed, and canvas filled. A thin wooden cap running along the outside top edge of the unit like a small gunwale will cover the seam. Before painting, caulking or bedding compound should be worked in along the bottom edge of the sponson where it meets the hull.

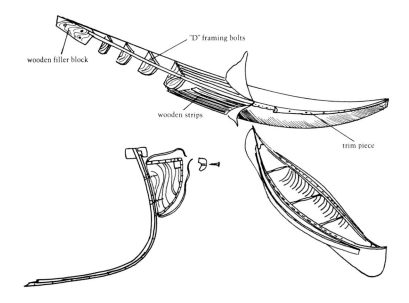

"D" framing bolts

wooden filler block

wooden strips

trim piece

just from being banged around. If a splice for a new section is required, I make sure the splice is at least 12″ long, spanning three or four ribs. It's a good idea to cut the rail back far enough so the splice doesn't fall in an area where the rail has to be bent. The ungainly rail is very difficult to handle when it's off the canoe, and it is easy to break a good rail if care isn't taken.

The Gerrish is just about complete. It's taken about 80 hours of my time, including the painting and varnishing over a six-week period. The extent of the repairs were typical of an older, severely damaged canoe, and of course, I did go to extra lengths to ensure the historical accuracy of the repairs, something that doesn't have to be done all the time. Many canoes require only a fraction of this amount of work.

Rips and tears in the canvas can happen to any canoe regardless of its age. A good patch on the canvas will last as long as the rest of the canvas; while the patch should not be obvious, it will never be completely hidden. The rip should be thoroughly dry and the area around it sanded to remove the paint and expose the canvas weave. A patch of fine cotton cloth similar in thickness of a T-shirt is cut so it is about 1-2″ wider than the tear. The damaged area receives a coating of waterproof glue similar to ambroid glue. Most hardware stores carry ambroid glue in tubes similar to airplane glue tubes. Saturate the cloth with the glue and apply it to the tear. After the glue is dry, several more coats of glue should be added until the weave and edges are completely filled with glue. The ambroid glue dries quite rapidly, and several coats can be applied and dried in an hour. The rough edges can be sanded smooth and the area painted. Any time the hull has five or six patches, it indicates the canvas is too weak or brittle to be functional and needs to be competely replaced — or indicates that someone needs canoeing lessons. I saw one canoe where a new sheet of canvas was glued completely over the old canoe canvas. It was effective for many years, but it certainly made the boat heavy.

Once in awhile a broken rib needs to be strengthened without the advantage of removing the canvas. The most effective method is to place a 12″ to 16″ section of rib stock right over the broken section and glue and screw it in place to the old rib with ⅝″ No.6 flat-head bronze wood screws. There are several methods of completely removing the old broken rib and installing a new rib without removing the canvas, but they are fairly complicated and don't really make a satisfactory or permanent repair.

An effective reinforcement of a small section of broken planking between two ribs is a metal patch. Force the splintered wood back into place and cut a section of sheet aluminum or brass (similar in thickness to alumninum houseflashing) that is about 3″ longer than the break and just about ½″ wider than the space between the two ribs. The area of the break is given a thin coating of bedding or caulking compound, and the metal patch is forced under the edges of the ribs over the broken planking. No fastenings are required. The tops of tin cans about the size of a soup can used to be a very popular material for planking repair.

One of the small items that I use a lot of is sandpaper. I find using a worn piece of sandpaper as effective as beating my head against the wall. Every step of every piece of work calls for some sort of sanding, and a good assortment of quality sandpaper is worth its weight in gold. Any piece of wood should be smoothed to at least 80 grit before it is installed. Installing a piece of wood straight from the saw or planer is certainly much faster, but why go to so much effort to restore or repair a functional canoe just to have poor finished results. It is always much easier and better to start with a coarse sandpaper and go through a series of finer grits than it is to try getting similar results by extra sanding with the fine sandpaper only.

What's a canoe worth? What's the Gerrish worth now? Eighty hours of labor, several hundred dollars in materials, and no cost for the basic hull. This would be about the same cost as for a good new wood canoe, $1,400. A new canoe would be more durable and a new plastic canoe can be had for $600, so why bother? What value is the canoe's history, its character, its spirit? The answer does not come from the head but from the heart.

Methods for strengthening a broken rib or repairing a small area of broken planking with a metal patch.

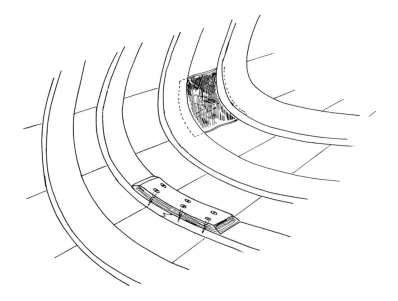

Canoe Maintenance

Wooden canoe maintenance is not the awesome job that most people envision. It does entail a small degree of commitment, but it is not a time- and money-consuming monster that makes a person regret he owns the canoe. A wood canoe will absorb a lot more abuse, punishment, rocks, and thundering rapids than most people give it credit for, but what it can't withstand is neglect. It can't be thrown in the backyard and forgotton until next summer, then dragged to the water and left neglected on the beach.

The two major rules to keep the canoe in good shape are to keep it dry and out of the sun when not in use. During the canoeing season it's going to be exposed to the elements, but when it's not in use it should be set up on some sawhorses or logs, in the shade of a building or tree. When the season is over, if it can't be taken into the garage or other storage area, all that is needed is a waterproof tarp secured around it. Heavy accumulations of snow can easily misshape or even crush a canoe, so snow should periodically be brushed off.

If covered storage cannot be obtained for the winter, all that is needed is to raise the canoe off the ground and wrap it with a good waterproof covering.

Before the canoe is to be used in the summer, take a look and see what needs to be touched up. The rails take a lot of abuse from canoe racks and paddles, and it is not uncommon for them to require a light sanding and one or two coats of varnish. The interior of the canoes used by professional guides may need to be revarnished each year, but most canoes won't need revarnishing for five to ten years. If the old varnish hasn't been cracked from age or too many old varnish coats, it's a simple matter of washing out the canoe, giving it a light hand-sanding, and brushing on one or two coats of high-gloss varnish. Scratches in the paint are only cosmetic and don't seriously affect the durability of the canoe. Scratches and gouges that are deep enough to dig into the canvas filler or expose the canvas weave are more serious and should be attended to at least once a year — or more often if the canoe is frequently used. The oil-base canvas filler that was orginally used on the canoe makes a poor filling agent over the old cured filler or paint. Small scrapes can be filled with several coats of ambroid glue. For larger and deeper gouges, a two-part plastic auto body filling compound is best. The filler is squeezed into the gouge with a putty knife, allowed to dry, then sanded smooth. It does not have to be painted over if you don't mind the odd colors that the auto body fillers seem to come in.

Painting the hull is not something that is required each year. Not only does each layer of paint add a surprising amount of weight, but many coats of paint will peel, flake, and crack sooner than a thin layer. Spot touch-ups of the paint should be adequate for many years. Exposure to the sun accelerates the checking of the paint, and once the surface is checked it is very difficult or impossible to obtain a smooth surface again without stripping the paint and starting over. The addition of one or two coats of new paint will do very little to cover existing cracks. Auto body filler can be used to fill the cracks but if the surface is checking because of age, it will continue to check in new areas and ruin any new paint job. The only sure way to get rid of a checked surface is to strip it off and remove the paint down to the canvas filler. Care must be taken when removing the paint by either sanding or chemical remover not to gouge, dig, or scrape away the canvas filler or expose the canvas weave. Again, small areas of canvas that are exposed can be treated with the body filler, but the plastic is not flexible enough to be used over large areas. Wet-and-dry sandpaper works best on the exterior paint, washing it off with water as you work. The paint doesn't clog the sandpaper, and there is no paint dust to contend with. If possible, it is best to use the same brand of paint that was

originally used. When mixing brands of paint there is always the possibility of them not being compatible, causing the new paint to peel or blister. It doesn't happen very often, but it is highly discouraging when it does. A high-gloss paint gives the most professional appearance; however, it also shows all the surface imperfections. A flat or even semi-gloss finish paint is easier to apply and hides many of those surface imperfections.

The most important preventative maintenance items are padded canoe racks for storage and transportation. Probably as much damage has been done to wooden canoes during storage or transportation as during actual use. The very best padding, as well as the longest lasting, is the half-round (in cross section) rubber foam enclosed in a heavy canvas sheathing. It is sold by marine dealers usually for protection around docks and floats.

If you keep up with the small nicks and scratches that beset your wood-canvas canoe, and store and transport it carefully, you will enjoy long periods of pleasure between major overhauls.

A good roof rack is worth its weight in gold.

Old Town Canoe

By 1900 the Gray family of Old Town, Maine, already had a history of successful entrepreneural ventures. The brothers — George, Herbert, and Wilbur — had been taught the values of hard work, self-reliance, and business acumen from their father, Alexander, and each operated his own business.

George started a canoe company in 1900 when he had Henry Wickett building canoes behind George's hardware store. The first four years saw a rapid growth in the canoe business, and in rapid succession it was known by the following names: Wickett Canvas, 1900; Indian Old Town Canoe, 1901-02; Robertson-Old Town Canoe 1902-04; and finally in 1904, the Old Town Canoe Company. When the company was first incorporated in 1902, Herbert Gray was president; George Richardson, a long-time Gray employee, treasurer; and J.R. Robertson, super-intendent. Robertson brought the rapidly growing company years of building experience from the Charles River region, but he was only with the company for a few years. George's son, Samuel, graduated from Bowdoin College in 1903 and he soon joined the company. Before long he became the daily manager of the plant, and in 1912 he assumed complete control of the company, which he held until his death in 1961.

When the four-story wood-frame Keith shoe factory was purchased in 1903, canoes were built on the first three floors and Bickmores Gall Cure was located on the top floor, but soon all the space was needed for canoe manufacture. In 1912 and 1914 major four- and five-story, 500'-long brick additions were added, giving the facilities over 150,000 square feet of floor space.

Until 1910 Old Town had its own crews in the woods harvesting, sawing, and sorting lumber for the plant but even the resources of Maine woods were not enough for the growing company. In the 1920s, the company began importing tight-grain, long-length Western red cedar for planking. Resilient Maine white cedar was still used for ribs. Native spruce and ash continued to be used for rails, stems, and thwarts, but Honduras mahogany became the standard for outside gunwales. During

"Old Town 'OTCA MODEL' Canoe"

A real Penobscot Indian Pageant in "Old Town Canoes"

The "Otca" model is the widest, deepest and roomiest. These features make it the steadiest, safest and most capacious canoe that we build. The floor is flat and wide, and carried far into the ends. The sides are convex, thus producing a handsome tumble-home. The 20″ long decks with low coaming or deck-end finish are practical, pleasing and distinctive. This model is not designed primarily for speed but for comfort, safety and fine appearance.

It is the sort of canoe one always takes pride in owning because of its true lines and details of fine craftsmanship. Equally at home on stream, lake or ocean, it never fails to give its owner and occupants a feeling of complete canoe joy.

The model is suited for use under any conditions anywhere. It paddles easily, will carry the largest load comfortably, can handle a maximum sail area. Illustrated with floor rack which is included in price of A. A. Grade but is $2.00 extra in C. S. Grade. Extras page 37. Stock Color Dark Green. Other colors, etc., pages 37 and following.

Length Extreme	Width Extreme	Depth Amidships	Approx. Weight	Approx. Weight Packed	For export (see note p. 32)		A. A. Grade (see p. 3) with keel		C. S. Grade (see p. 3) with keel	
					Approx. Weight Crated	Approx. Cubic Measurements	Open Mahogany Gunwales	Telegraph Code Word	Open Spruce Gunwales	Telegraph Code Word
16 ft.	34½ in.	13 in.	75 lbs.	130 lbs.	260 lbs.	125 ft.	$92.00	Otcam	$82.00	Otcaler
17 "	35 "	13 "	85 "	135 "	270 "	140 "	95.00	Otcapt	85.00	Otcasem
18 "	37 "	13 "	90 "	145 "	290 "	155 "	98.00	Otcarlet	88.00	Otcaret

In Writing Order, Give Length, Grade, Model, Color and Price. Also Extras and Equipment.

5

"Old Town 'H. W. MODEL' Canoe"

Instead of having a perfectly flat floor the H. W. Model tends toward the shape of the well-known salt water yawl boat below the water line. This shape gives more draft and hence greater steadiness in windy waters. It is a general utility model, somewhat faster under the paddle than the Otca Model, sturdy and handsome in appearance—the kind of canoe that is always ready for any use.

Extra fullness at bow and stern enables this model to ride over large waves instead of cutting through them as in the case of a canoe with sharp ends. For cruising, carrying heavy loads, for use on large rivers, lakes, ponds and salt water, this is an excellent canoe. The lines are speedy and graceful and the ends curve with that nicety given by the Indians to their bark canoes. It's a good sailer.

This H. W. Model has all the essentials in lines and quality to make any owner proud of his possession. All parts are shaped for lightness coupled with ample allowance for strength. There is no excess weight. Hunters and others who have portaging to do will appreciate this. Extras page 37. Stock Color Dark Green. Other colors, etc., pages 37 and following.

The boys are taking the picture

Length Extreme	Width Extreme	Depth Amidships	Approx. Weight	Approx. Weight Packed	For export (see note p. 32)		A. A. Grade (see p. 3) with keel		C. S. Grade (see p. 3) with keel	
					Approx. Weight Crated	Approx. Cubic Measurements	Open Mahogany Gunwales	Telegraph Code Word	Open Spruce Gunwales	Telegraph Code Word
16 ft.	33 in.	12 in.	70 lbs.	120 lbs.	260 lbs.	125 ft.	$88.00	Ahatching	$78.00	Ahealing
17 "	34 "	12 "	80 "	130 "	270 "	140 "	91.00	Aharboring	81.00	Ahectoring
18 "	34½ "	12½ "	85 "	140 "	290 "	150 "	94.00	Ahalting	84.00	Ahelping

In Writing Order, Give Length, Grade, Model, Color and Price. Also Extras and Equipment.

6

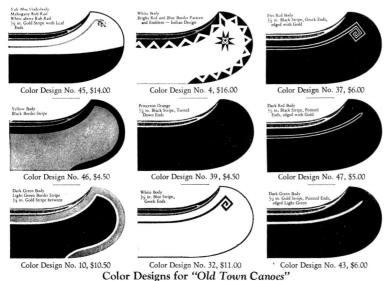

Yale Blue Underbody
Mahogany Rub Rail
White above Rub Rail
½ in. Gold Stripe with Leaf
Ends

Color Design No. 45, $14.00

White Body
Bright Red and Blue Border Pattern
and Emblem — Indian Design

Color Design No. 4, $16.00

Fire Red Body
½ in. Black Stripe, Greek Ends,
edged with Gold

Color Design No. 37, $6.00

Yellow Body
Black Border Stripe

Color Design No. 46, $4.50

Princeton Orange
½ in. Black Stripe, Turned
Down Ends

Color Design No. 39, $4.50

Dark Red Body
½ in. Black Stripe, Pointed
Ends, edged with Gold

Color Design No. 47, $5.00

Dark Green Body
Light Green Border Stripe
½ in. Gold Stripe between

Color Design No. 10, $10.50

White Body
½ in. Blue Stripe,
Greek Ends

Color Design No. 32, $11.00

Dark Green Body
½ in. Gold Stripe, Pointed Ends,
edged Light Green

' Color Design No. 43, $6.00

Color Designs for "Old Town Canoes"

These end sections show a wide range of designs for the whole length of the canoe. In ordering specify design number and price. Price is additional to cost of canoe. Designs are susceptible to various color schemes, and to any combination of colors you may submit. Price Design No. 45 includes mahogany rub rail ($5.00) which separates the colors. Assortment of these designs in stock but suggest allow ten days. Stripes priced page 37.

World War II, when imported materials were hard to obtain, Old Town was able to dust off its original logging equipment and once again sent crews in the woods to harvest lumber.

As soon as open-gunwale construction became popular around 1910, Old Town developed their distinctive diamond-headed bolts, now a well-known Old Town trademark.

Old Town Canoe was founded and nurtured by the business and leadership skills of the Gray family. Actual canoe-building skills were obtained by purchasing the right business or by hiring the right people. Henry Wickett, J.R. Robertson, and B.N. Morris (after fire destroyed his own respected business) were all experts recruited by Old Town at various times, and the Carleton Canoe Company was just one of the businesses acquired by Old Town to increase its own lines of canoes.

Samuel Gray's leadership and emphasis on quality made Old Town Canoe the world's leading canoe-building company until aluminum canoes became popular in the 1950s. The impact was stunning, nearly ruining the half-century-old company; at one point Grumman was selling 20,000 canoes a year, while Old Town produced only several hundred. In combination with the decline in business came a transition of control from Samuel to his sons, Braly and Deane. Samuel continued as head of the company until 1961 but for the last 10 years of that period, the plant was actually under the control of the two brothers. Braly retired in 1964, leaving Deane Gray with sole control of the company.

Deane tried to maintain the company's wooden canoe history, but economics forced the company to adopt the fiberglass and plastic technology of the early 1960s. With a fiberglass line, Old Town slowly began to increase sales and production with a greatly reduced labor force. The introduction of Royalex canvas in the early '70s accelerated the firm's recovery, and by 1975 the business was prosperous enough to be attractive to the Johnson Wax Company, another family-owned business expanding into the recreational market. Deane Gray stayed on as manager after the sale of the company that year to Johnson's, until his retirement in 1978.

In 1982, the current president, Ron Blass

from Minnesota, was brought in to oversee
the operation, and production and sales
have continued to rise steadily to around
the 10,000 canoe-per-year level.

In 1985, Old Town purchased the White
Canoe Company from owner Ed Soule,
maintaining the firm's identity as the
nation's oldest, still active canoe company,
and continuing to increase production of
fiberglass canoes under the White name.

Old Town continues to produce quality
wooden canoes; fiberglass is the standard
covering but canvas is still an option. The
bottom floor of the original factory
continues to house the wooden canoe
department, where Clark Michaud and a
small crew still build the canoes that made
Old Town famous. Clark learned wooden
canoe building from Joe Lavoie, who
started building wood-canvas canoes for
the White Canoe Company in 1948. Joe
recently retired after many years at Old
Town, however, he still comes in to work
on special canoe restorations.

Canoe Study Plans

The following study plans should acquaint the reader with a variety of canoe shapes drawn in all the views. The tables of offsets may be used to loft out the respective canoes, or simply to enlarge the cross sections to full size for mold patterns. However, deductions will have to be made for the combined thicknesses of the form, plus the ribs and planking of the canoe for a truly accurate form. This step may be skipped, but the resulting canoe will be correspondingly larger in volume than the original.

Construction plans for each of the canoes — which include plan, profile, and half-breadth views — are available. The plans include offsets as well as full-sized paper templates on separate sheets for each of the molds, corrected to result in an accurate canoe. Prices are IGWA&L, $30; Cheemaun, $35; and Atkinson Traveler, $40 postpaid, available from the authors at Northwoods Canoe Shop, RFD#3 Box 118-2A, Dover-Foxcroft, Maine 04426.